WITHDRAWN

Quinoa
365

Quinoa

THE EVERYDAY
SUPERFOOD

365

PATRICIA GREEN & CAROLYN HEMMING

whitecap

Whitecap Books is known for its expertise in the cookbook market, and has produced some of the most innovative and familiar titles found in kitchens across North America. Visit our website at www.whitecap.ca.

Edited by Elaine Jones
Proofread by Paula Ayer
Interior design and illustrations by Setareh Ashrafologhalai
Food photography by Ryan Szulc
Food styling by Nancy Midwicki
Prop styling by Madeleine Johari

Printed in China

Library and Archives Canada Cataloguing in Publication

Green, Patricia
    Quinoa 365 : the everyday superfood / Patricia Green & Carolyn Hemming.

Includes index.
ISBN 978-1-55285-994-0

    1. Cookery (Quinoa). I. Hemming, Carolyn II. Title. III. Title: Quinoa three hundred sixty-five.

TX393G74 2010   641.6'31   C2009-906413-8

The publisher acknowledges the financial support of the Government of Canada through the Canada Book Fund (CBF) and the Province of British Columbia through the Book Publishing Tax Credit.

10 11 12 13 14 5 4 3 2 1

We dedicate this book to our mom, Vera E. Friesen,
for always stressing the food-as-medicine principle
and for her lasting influence on us about the
importance of health and wellness.

CONTENTS

· Preface   viii

· Introduction   1

· The Mystery & History of Quinoa   9
by Claire Burnett, MSc, and Laurie Scanlin, PhD

1   EVERYDAY SUPER STARTS   11
Quinoa for Breakfast

2   EVERYDAY STAPLES   33
Appetizers, Sides, Snacks & Salads

3   EVERYDAY SOUPS & STEWS   57
Healthful & Hearty

4   EVERYDAY ENTRÉES   79
For Both Carnivores & Vegetarians!

5   EVERYDAY TREATS   123
Cookies, Muffins & More

6   EVERYDAY DESSERTS   153
Satisfy Your Sweet Tooth

7   EVERYDAY BABY FOOD *with* QUINOA   181
Nutritious Beginnings

· Index   192

· Acknowledgments   198

PREFACE

While she was inverted in some knotted-up yoga pose, my mother would remind us, as we walked through the front door, that our after-school snack of seaweed chips was waiting for us on the kitchen counter. We would grumble to ourselves—we wished we had regular snacks like other kids. Brought up on strictly homemade baking, we would shamelessly stare at the white bread our classmates devoured at lunch, thinking that surely it must taste better; after all, their perfectly symmetrical white sandwiches certainly *looked* better. Our sandwiches were rough, the heavy brown slabs of bread thick, unevenly cut and full of ominous, buglike grains.

But we began to appreciate the uniqueness of our healthful home when friends cringed with horror at our stinky dried seaweed and brown seedy bread. Somehow their fear made the chips taste better and the bread sweeter, and we began to feel like we belonged to some secret organization. As adults looking back, we appreciate even more all those times when Mom gently held our chins so she could dump the tablespoon of cod liver oil into our resistant mouths. We laugh, remembering that Santa would never have dared slip a book on the health benefits of garlic into a teenager's Christmas stocking.

As prairie girls, our closeness to nature and the land was shaped by weekends at Grandma and Grandpa's farm, us running wild through the grain, snooping for treasure in the barn and seeing who could catch the most field mice darting among the granaries. Like it or not, we were raised with the constant awareness that the land provides life. When Grandma would send us out with instructions to return with heaping pails of berries, we simply knew that nothing could be better for us than the natural goodness of whole food.

Although I have always been a picky eater, as the younger sister I would often take the guidance of my only sister, Patricia. If a particular food I was unsure of was okay with her, I would be more likely to taste it. As an adult, my healthful habits persevered, but I was not interested in taking time to make an entire meal, content instead to eat old-fashioned oatmeal, cottage cheese or plain yogurt and muesli every day.

Eventually, Patricia convinced me that quinoa could provide the diversity, energy and protein I needed for my physical workouts and hectic workweek. And it was easy to cook! I began to consume quinoa voraciously. Thrilled with the ease of cooking, I began making large batches on the weekends for my breakfasts, lunches and dinners, while Patricia invented new and exciting ways to prepare quinoa and sneak it into the daily meals she fed her energetic children and hard-working husband. Her adventurous experimentation and insistence on creating great-tasting meals with the most nutritional impact, and my critical eating habits, have led to our compiling our recipes in this book.

Quinoa 365 will show you that incorporating healthy alternatives into your everyday lifestyle is simple when you use quinoa. The versatility of this superfood makes it easy to bridge the gap between already established eating habits and increasingly nutritious food choices.

Here you will find a bit of the history and nutritional characteristics of quinoa, along with everyday recipes that work well with quinoa, including breakfast ideas, salads, appetizers, snacks, sides, soups and stews, meat and vegetarian dishes, gluten-free dishes, cookies, muffins, loaves, scrumptious desserts and even baby food. For those special occasions, or for just another weekday dinner, you will find a quinoa recipe to please. The quick breakfast smoothies, hearty casseroles, decadent chocolate cookies and more will be sure to satisfy your family and friends. —CH

INTRODUCTION

Essentials of Quinoa

Once considered an alternative crop or a niche food, quinoa is now becoming increasingly common in North America. Interest in the superior nutritional properties of quinoa (a food previously common only among vegetarians or the gluten-intolerant) has encouraged cooks at all skill levels to create unique dishes to please themselves and their families and intrigue dinner party guests. Nutrient-packed quinoa has sparked the interest of the health-conscious, those seeking weight loss and those on high-protein diets.

Although quinoa is mostly grown in South America, you will find it on most grocery store shelves, and in health food stores and bulk food warehouses. You can also order quinoa online from health food supply stores, making it easy to get larger quantities shipped right to your front door. Pastas that use quinoa as an ingredient, often combined with rice, kamut or potato flours, can also be found on the market.

If you've got 15 minutes, you have time to cook quinoa. It cooks up in a snap and lasts in the refrigerator for up to one week. Tight for time? Preparing plain quinoa on the weekend and leaving it in the refrigerator will allow you to speedily throw together many of your favorite recipes in no time at all. You can use quinoa in almost everything, which means you can eat it for breakfast, lunch, dinner and snacks—and get maximum health benefits from this superfood.

Those who are familiar with quinoa tend to cook it in a few of their favorite, standard quinoa dishes. Others have only recently learned about it and have many questions about how to cook quinoa and incorporate it into their daily menus. Whether you're a dabbler in the kitchen or an experienced cook, these recipes will show you how to use this valuable superfood every day.

ECONOMICS OF QUINOA

Quinoa may seem a little expensive at $3 to $4 per pound ($6–8 per kg), but because it cooks up to three or more times its original volume, it provides more nutritional value and energy than comparable amounts of white rice, pasta or meat. To give some perspective, compare it to these grocery items we commonly buy: American cheddar cheese, $1 to $2 per pound ($3–4 per kg); kidney beans, $0.30 per pound ($0.60 per kg); butter, $3 per pound ($6 per kg); coffee, $8 to $10 per pound ($16–20 per kg).

Quinoa is high in vitamins and minerals such as riboflavin, calcium, vitamin E, iron, potassium, phosphorus, magnesium, folic acid and beta carotene.[1] In 1 cup (250 mL) of regular uncooked white quinoa, there are 626 calories, with a whopping 24 g protein!

1 cup (250 mL) uncooked quinoa	
Calories	626
Total fat	10 g
Saturated fat	1 g
Trans fat	0 g
Cholesterol	0 mg
Sodium	8 mg
Total carbohydrate	109 g
Dietary fiber	12 g
Protein	24 g

1 cup (250 mL) cooked quinoa	
Calories	222
Total fat	3.5 g
Saturated fat	0 g
Trans fat	0 g
Cholesterol	0 mg
Sodium	13 mg
Total carbohydrate	40 g
Dietary fiber	5 g
Protein	8 g

Source: Data from Nutrient Data Laboratory. Retrieved September 2, 2009, from the USDA National Nutrient Database: http://www.nal.usda.gov/fnic/foodcomp/search/index.html.

Identified as one of the world's healthiest foods, quinoa has a complete combination of all life-supporting nutrients, making it an ideal whole food to incorporate into your daily lifestyle. The versatility of quinoa makes it compatible with almost everything you eat throughout the year. Soups, salads, entrées and desserts can all be made with quinoa and taste great. It is very easy to prepare, regardless of your cooking ability. Quinoa is also considered kosher, as it is technically not a grain nor related to grains.

Especially important for vegetarians or vegans, quinoa is a nutritionally superior source of non-animal protein. Optimal amino acid content and ease of digestion make quinoa an ideal alternative to meat proteins.

Those on weight-loss diets can also benefit from quinoa, which is a complex carbohydrate, also known as a "good" carbohydrate. Unlike simple carbohydrates from processed foods, quinoa digests gradually. This contributes more nutritional value because it does not quickly convert sugar to fat, making it ideal for low-carbohydrate diets. In addition, complex carbohydrates leave you feeling fuller longer and can help to regulate blood sugar levels. Some research has shown that high-protein diets may aid in weight loss.[2] High levels of protein may be beneficial for weight loss, but if the primary protein source is fatty meats, you could create additional health concerns. Red meat, in particular, contains saturated fat, and excessive consumption of saturated fats has been shown to cause heart disease. Many meats also contain antibiotics, additives and preservatives. For those on a high-protein diet, quinoa makes an ideal meat substitute.

Quinoa has been ranked as one of the top ten muscle-building foods for its protein, amino acid content and complex carbohydrates.[3] The quality of protein in quinoa means that the body efficiently uses the building blocks, rather than eliminating them as waste as with many of the protein supplements that muscle building requires. Quinoa is also an ideal athletic-performance food because the complex carbohydrates provide energy and endurance to hard-working muscles.

A growing number of people have allergies to food, including wheat and wheat derivatives and even foods containing traces of wheat. Quinoa does not belong to the same plant family as wheat and does not contain gluten. It is therefore safe for the gluten-intolerant or those

---

1 Eskin, M., *Quinoa: Properties and Performance* (Kamsack, Saskatchewan: Shaw Printers, 2002), 5–12.
2 Adams, M., "High protein diet good for your health, good for weight loss, says startling new research," *Natural News*, http://www.naturalnews.com/001480.html (retrieved August 17, 2008).
3 Kalman, D., "The Top 10 Muscle Building Foods," *ProSource*, 2007, http://www.prosource.net/article-2007-top-10-muscle-building-foods.jsp (retrieved August 17, 2008).

The ancient Incas called quinoa "the mother grain" for a reason. This whole food was thought to promote healthy pregnancy, contribute to a healthy baby and enhance a mother's milk. Quinoa is rich in the amino acid histadine, which cannot be formed by combinations of nutrients and instead must be provided directly in the diet. Histadine is considered an essential amino acid in children because it is necessary for human development.[10] The perfect profile of quinoa's nutrients is ideal for providing a great start to children.

Quinoa offers abundant protein that is easily digestible. It is almost always organic and full of fiber, iron and calcium, which are three key components for baby nutrition as defined by the United States Department of Agriculture (USDA) and Canadian nutritional requirements. Quinoa is a great alternative to traditional "first" foods that have inferior nutrient value, such as rice. The increasing incidence of allergies to dairy and wheat can be safely avoided with the choice of quinoa.

with celiac disease, Crohn's disease or colitis. Quinoa has been identified as ideal for the gluten-free diets recommended for autistic children and those with Attention Deficit Disorder (ADD).[4]

Quinoa, while not technically a grain, is similar to whole grains, which have been demonstrated to reduce high blood pressure and prevent heart failure because they slow the speed of arterial plaque and may help to remove buildup of plaque in the arteries.[5] Quinoa is also rich in magnesium, which helps to reduce high blood pressure because it allows the blood vessels to relax. In addition, plant lignans, or phytonutrients, are present in whole foods such as quinoa and are thought to be responsible for protection against a variety of illnesses.

Even beyond heart health, consumption of whole grains has been linked to a decreased risk of breast cancer,[6] prevention of gallstones[7] and a lower risk of type 2 diabetes.[8] Quinoa's high manganese and copper content gives it antioxidant power to promote the elimination of toxins and free radicals that may cause disease. It is also abundant in linolenic acid, the essential fatty acid that has proven beneficial to immune response.[9]

This is indeed a superfood!

Types of Quinoa

Quinoa seeds (often referred to as "grains") are available in red, black, and white or a golden color. White or golden are the most common available commercially, with black and red becoming increasingly available. The colors can be mixed together in recipes, or used to create drama in dishes for special occasions. The recipes in this book, unless specified, mostly use white or golden quinoa, but you can experiment with any colors you choose. The nutritional values of different colors may vary slightly; however, they all are power-packed.

Processed **quinoa flour** is a creamy ivory color and most often has the same fine texture as regular all-purpose flour. However, some quinoa flours on the market are more rustic and have a coarser texture. We suggest you buy the finest one available for the best baking results.

4 Gates, D., "Understanding the Inner Ecosystem & Unlocking the Mystery of Autism," http://bodyecology.com/autism.php (retrieved January 21, 2009).

5 Djousse, L. and J. Gaziano, "Breakfast cereals and risk of heart failure in the physicians' health study I," *Archives of Internal Medicine* 167, no. 19 (Oct 22, 2007): 2080–5.

6 Cade, J.E., V.J. Burley and D.C. Greenwood, "Dietary fibre and risk of breast cancer in the UK Women's Cohort Study," *International Journal of Epidemiology*, January 24, 2007.

7 Tsai, C., M. Leitzmann et al., "Long-term intake of dietary fiber and decreased risk of cholecystectomy in women," *American Journal of Gastroenterology* 99, no. 7 (July 2004): 1364–70.

8 van Dam, R., F. Hu et al, "Dietary calcium and magnesium, major food sources, and risk of type 2 diabetes in U.S. Black women," *Diabetes Care* 29, no. 10 (October 2006): 2238–43.

9 Eskin, *Quinoa: Properties and Performance*, 23.

10 "Histadine," *Encyclopaedia Britannica* online, http://www.britannica.com/EBchecked/topic/267029/histadine (retrieved February 20, 2009).

Quinoa cultivation is thought to have many advantages over other crops. Extremely hardy, the 5- to 6-foot (1.5 to 1.8 m) quinoa plant's ability to germinate in cool temperatures and grow at high elevations in droughtlike conditions makes it an extremely dependable crop. Also worth noting is that an astonishing 4 cups (1 L) of quinoa seed will grow an entire acre of crop! In addition, the saponin seed coating provides an all-natural, safe pesticide for protection of the crop without the use of chemicals.

RINSING QUINOA

The light, nutty and sometimes slightly bitter flavor of quinoa is a result of the protective coating, called saponin, on the outside of the seed. Most of it is washed off during commercial processing, so unless you're buying quinoa from a local farmer or in bulk, the saponin will already be removed. Regardless, some insist that the taste of cooked quinoa is further improved if it is rinsed before it is prepared. This can be done by rinsing quinoa under running water in a strainer or soaking the quinoa in a bowl for two to three hours and then rinsing it. In addition, while rinsing or soaking the quinoa you can gently rub it between your fingers to quickly rid it of any remaining bitterness. If you are at all concerned about any bitter taste of the quinoa you have purchased, these steps will remove it.

If you prefer a coarse texture, however, you can also make your own flour by grinding raw quinoa in a blender or food processor.

Quinoa flour has a nutty flavor that some might consider slightly bitter. Paired with the proper ingredients, the slight bitterness disappears and the result is great taste and the knowledge that the dish you've prepared is super nutritious. Quinoa flour can be used in almost all regular baking, but the slightly nutty flavor may alter the final taste of your dish. This flavor works well in most recipes, but may occasionally overpower in others. In addition, the lack of gluten can make your quick breads feel slightly denser and heavier. An option when incorporating quinoa flour into your baking is to use a portion of quinoa flour, combined with portions of all-purpose white, whole wheat, potato, tapioca or rice flours. Store quinoa flour in the refrigerator or freezer for maximum freshness.

Quinoa flakes are available in health food stores and some specialty grocery stores. They have the same texture as rolled oats and are prepared similarly. As with cooked oatmeal, the taste of quinoa flakes is fairly plain so they are easily compatible with many of the same recipes as oats. Quinoa flakes make a great breakfast cereal and can be combined with dried apricots, raisins or fresh fruit; flakes also make a fantastic baby food. It is sometimes a challenge to find quinoa flakes on the market, so we have included only a few recipes with flakes in this book.

Preparing Quinoa

Quinoa is easy to cook and a variety of methods can be used. Simply choose the one that works best for you.

Quinoa cooks much like rice, couscous or millet and can be used in many of the same dishes. Cooked quinoa fluffs up and expands the same way as rice and almost triples the original uncooked amount. The natural nutty flavor is complemented by fruit, vegetables, sauces, meats—almost everything you prepare already, every day. Quinoa's versatility means that you can use it in appetizers and side dishes or as an entrée all on its own. It is a thickening agent and makes a superb soup base or pudding, whether you use the seeds puréed or the flour cooked in water.

SIMMER AND SET. The main method of preparing quinoa is the stovetop simmer-and-set method, which is similar to cooking rice. Quinoa cooks in half the time it takes to cook rice, with one cup cooking in roughly 10 to 15 minutes. The simmer-and-set method is our preferred method because it's quick and no draining is required.

QUINOA SPROUTS

Prefer to eat your food alive? Sprouted, living foods are rich in enzymes, and many believe that eating sprouted grains can increase energy, cleanse the body, speed healing and lead to optimal heath. Sprouted grains can be eaten alone or added to cold foods such as salads and sandwiches.

To sprout quinoa, place the seeds in a shallow dish of water. Germination happens rapidly, and from the time the tiny germ uncurls from the seed, the sprouted quinoa is ready to eat. The sprouts taste best when left to grow for about 12 to 14 hours (see page 56 for complete method). The final quantity of sprouts will depend on the duration of the sprouting process.

Raw Quinoa	Water	Sprouted Quinoa (approximate)
2 Tbsp (30 mL)	½ cup (125 mL)	⅓ cup (80 mL)
¼ cup (60 mL)	¾ cup (185 mL)	¾ cup (185 mL)
⅓ cup (80 mL)	1 cup (250 mL)	1 cup (250 mL)
½ cup (125 mL)	1½ cups (625 mL)	1½ cups (625 mL)
⅔ cup (160 mL)	2 cups (500 mL)	2 cups (500 mL)
¾ cup (185 mL)	2¼ cups (560 mL)	2¼ cups (560 mL)
1 cup (250 mL)	3 cups (750 mL)	3 cups (750 mL)

Cook the quinoa by combining the quinoa and water and bringing to a boil. Cover, reduce to a simmer and cook for 10 minutes. Then turn the heat off, keeping the saucepan covered and on the burner to allow residual heat in the pot to continue cooking the quinoa for another 4 to 7 minutes. The amount of time it sits covered depends on how it will be used. If the desired texture is al dente, such as in salads, allow 4 to 5 minutes. Where a lighter, plumper and fluffier texture of quinoa is required, such as in breakfast cereals and most entrées, allow the saucepan to sit covered for 5 to 7 minutes. For recipes such as baby food and baking, the saucepan should sit covered for 10 to 15 minutes.

There's no need to stir or lift the cover during the cooking process, but remember to remove from the heat and uncover after the set period to prevent overcooking. If water still remains after the appropriate cooking time, it's likely a result of covering the saucepan and decreasing the temperature before bringing to a full boil. To solve this, leave the saucepan covered on the burner for an additional 5 minutes. Red and black quinoa may leave a small amount of water if the total cooking time is less than 14 minutes. Excess water can easily be drained off.

YIELDS		
Uncooked Quinoa	Water (or other liquid, not including milk)	Cooked Quinoa (approximate)
2 Tbsp (30 mL)	¼ cup (60 mL)	⅓ cup (80 mL)
¼ cup (60 mL)	½ cup (125 mL)	¾ cup (185 mL)
⅓ cup (80 mL)	⅔ cup (160 mL)	1 cup (250 mL)
½ cup (125 mL)	1 cup (250 mL)	1½ cups (375 mL)
⅔ cup (160 mL)	1⅓ cups (330 mL)	2 cups (500 mL)
¾ cup (185 mL)	1½ cups (375 mL)	2¼ cups (560 mL)
1 cup (250 mL)	2 cups (500 mL)	3 cups (750 mL)

COOK AND DRAIN. A great method for those concerned about any potential bitter taste, this method is the same as cooking pasta. Cook the quinoa uncovered in a large saucepan of water on medium-high heat for about 15 minutes. (Use about four parts water to one part quinoa.) Drain well; the quinoa will be translucent and plump. Uncooked quinoa will yield the same cooked amounts as above.

STEAMER. Quinoa can be steamed in any of the convenient and popular rice steamers available on the market; simply follow the manufacturer's instructions for cooking white rice, and remember to leave extra room for the additional volume of quinoa.

SLOW COOKER. Quinoa can be added to slow-cooker recipes such as soups, chilies and casseroles. To add quinoa, ensure you have enough liquid: 2 cups (500 mL) for every 1 cup (250 mL) of quinoa. Add the quinoa halfway through the total cooking time.

We don't recommend cooking quinoa in a microwave oven as it requires more time and attention and doesn't consistently result in a light, fluffy texture.

How to Use This Book

All of the recipes in this book can be enjoyed by anyone. Most of them can be made with or without meat, dairy or gluten using any of the alternatives normally suited for these types of menus. Look for the following symbols, which indicate the recipe is gluten-free, kid-approved and/or vegetarian. Take care to use the appropriate ingredients where necessary.

Gluten-Free

A recipe with this symbol means it does not contain products derived from gluten-containing cereal grains including wheat, rye or barley (or that it is gluten-free when made with the specified alternate ingredients). We suggest buying ingredients such as baking powder and oats that are labeled gluten-free.

Kid-Approved

The recipe has been tested and given a "thumbs-up" by children.

Vegetarian

The recipe does not contain fish, chicken or meat (but may contain dairy or eggs). If fish, chicken or meat is listed in the recipe, it isn't integral to the dish and can be eliminated to make the dish vegetarian.

The Mystery & History of Quinoa

by Claire Burnett, MSc, and Laurie Scanlin, PhD
Vice president and president of Keen Ingredients Inc.

Quinoa is believed to be the most powerful food to come from the Andean Mountain regions of Peru and Bolivia. Over five thousand years ago the indigenous peoples of the Altiplano regarded quinoa as more valuable than gold. The Incas considered quinoa to be their most sacred food, which contained spiritually enhancing qualities, and so named it *la chisiya mama*, or "the mother grain." At the start of each growing season, the emperor would perform elaborate religious rituals to ensure a prosperous crop and then give thanks at harvest. Celebrations often included the consumption of a fermented beerlike quinoa beverage called *chicha*.

The Incas found that only quinoa was powerful enough to sustain their bodies and provide them with the stamina, strength and energy required to perform endurance activities. The Inca armies would march for days and even weeks at altitudes above twelve thousand feet, consuming absolutely no animal protein. Their only source of nutrition and energy came from a mixture of quinoa and fat referred to as "war balls."

The quinoa seed contains a bitter coating called *saponin*, which is normally removed prior to consumption. Saponin has an undesirable taste, making it an effective means of protecting the plant from attack by insects and birds. The majority of saponin is removed by means of mechanical abrasion prior to distribution, but it is still recommended that quinoa be rinsed before using to wash off any remaining bitterness. The saponin byproduct has potential industrial uses, including natural insecticides, soaps and shampoos, and is being investigated for its possible pharmaceutical uses.

When the Spanish arrived in the 1500s, they recognized the strength that quinoa brought to the Incas. In order to control their culture, the Spanish armies destroyed the quinoa fields and made it illegal for the Incas to grow, consume or worship the "magical" grain. Quinoa was replaced with crops such as potatoes, wheat and barley, and soon after, malnutrition and infant mortality were on the rise. What little quinoa cultivation remained was hidden away high up on the mountainous hillsides, where the plant adapted to the harsh environmental extremes of poor soil, drought, intense ultraviolet light and severe frost. Its superior nutritional qualities, adaptation to harsh conditions and ability to survive for over five thousand years have earned quinoa the right to be called a true *superfood*.

Quinoa is still cultivated and commercially grown in Peru and Bolivia, but its range has stretched to include Ecuador, Chile, Colombia, Argentina and, more recently, Colorado, Canada, Asia and even Europe. Quinoa's popularity today comes not only from its heartiness and ability to grow in marginal conditions, but also from its superior nutritional composition.

Continued on next page . . .

Superfood—Super Nutrition

Today, quinoa is most frequently consumed in its whole form, but it's also available as flour and as flakes. As a commercial ingredient, quinoa is gaining popularity and can be occasionally found in pasta, nutrition bars, baked goods and cereals.

Technically, quinoa is not a grain at all. It is cultivated and used similarly to a grain but is actually the fruit of a broadleaf plant. It is in the same family as spinach and beets (*Chenopodiaceae*) and is classified as a "pseudocereal." The seeds range in color from ivory to magenta, yellow, orange, red, green, brown and even black. Some quinoa fields are grown strictly for one color preference, while others exhibit the full rainbow of its spectacular colors.

The protein in quinoa is the source of its power. It contains all of the essential amino acids necessary to support human growth and development. According to the Food and Agriculture Organization (FAO) of the United Nations, the nutritional quality of quinoa compares to that of dried whole milk. Extremely rare for a vegetable or plant, quinoa's amino acid composition is of higher quality than wheat, barley, rice or soybeans and is comparable to casein, the protein found in milk.

Most grains are limited in the amino acid *lysine*, while legumes are limited in the amino acids *cysteine* and *methionine*. Since these foods are considered to be incomplete, it's necessary to eat a variety of them to ensure adequate protein. Quinoa, however, is classified as a complete protein. Additionally, quinoa is gluten-free, is hypoallergenic and contains substantial amounts of the amino acid *histidine*, which is essential for infants and young children. (Quinoa has long been used as a weaning food for babies in the Andean regions.)

Not to be overlooked is the vitamin and mineral content of quinoa. It is rich in vitamins E, B2 and B6, folic acid, biotin, calcium, potassium, iron, copper, magnesium, manganese and chloride. Quinoa is higher in calcium and iron than rice, corn, wheat, barley or oats.

Research has shown the oil component in quinoa, when compared to corn, sesame, soybean and cottonseed, has lower levels of saturated fat and higher levels of mono-and polyunsaturated fats. It is free of cholesterol and trans fat. The fatty acid composition of quinoa oil is similar to that of corn, with a high concentration of linoleic and linolenic acid. Additionally, quinoa contains high levels of natural antioxidants, mainly tocopherols (vitamin E), recognized to have cancer-preventative and anti-aging effects. Antioxidants also help prevent rancidity, which leads to a natural extension of the product's shelf life.

For all these reasons, NASA is considering quinoa as a crop for Controlled Ecological Life Support System (CELSS). Initial studies by NASA indicate that it could be an excellent crop for CELSS because of its high concentration of protein, ease of use, versatility in preparation and potential for high crop yields. In the future, quinoa may be feeding our astronauts on their long journey to Mars.

Chapter 1

EVERYDAY SUPER STARTS

Quinoa for Breakfast

Your breakfast routine just got better. Kick-start your morning and energize your entire day with the endurance power of quinoa. If you enjoy a hot breakfast, try our Raisin Pudding Breakfast Porridge, an omelet or waffles. Breakfast on the go is also easy with the Tropical Beach Smoothie or Strawberry Shake. The Pumpkin Pancakes, one of our breakfast favorites, also make a great cold snack!

Serves 1.

Serves 1.

Apple Strudel
Breakfast Cereal

The taste of sweet, layered strudel—without the pastry.

¼ cup (60 mL) slivered almonds
1 cup (250 mL) quinoa
2½ cups (625 mL) water
½ cup (125 mL) diced dried apple slices
¼ cup (60 mL) raisins
1 tsp (5 mL) ground cinnamon
1 tsp (5 mL) pure vanilla extract
1 Tbsp (15 mL) brown sugar (optional)
1 cup (250 mL) vanilla yogurt

Place the almonds in a medium saucepan over medium-high heat. Stir frequently until the almonds are toasted and fragrant, about 3 to 4 minutes. Set the almonds aside in a small bowl.

Combine the quinoa, water, apple, raisins and cinnamon in the same saucepan. Bring to a boil, cover and reduce to a simmer for 17 minutes. Stir in the vanilla and brown sugar (if using). To serve, divide between bowls, top with vanilla yogurt and sprinkle with toasted almonds.

Blueberry Flax Hot Cereal

This wholesome, hot breakfast cereal has the perfect combination of flavor and nutrients. You can substitute old-fashioned rolled oats for the quick-cooking oats; just add them to the mixture after seven minutes of cooking time. This recipe can easily be made in double or triple quantities.

⅔ cup (160 mL) water
3 Tbsp (45 mL) quinoa
2 Tbsp (30 mL) quick-cooking rolled oats
1–2 tsp (5–10 mL) maple syrup, honey or brown sugar
1½ tsp (7.5 mL) flax (ground or whole seeds)
2 Tbsp (30 mL) blueberries, fresh (or frozen and thawed)
Milk, half and half cream or vanilla yogurt (optional)

Place the water and quinoa in a small saucepan, bring to a boil and cover. Reduce to a simmer and cook for 10 minutes. Stir in the oats, cover and continue to cook for another 5 minutes, until the oats are tender. Remove from the heat. Stir in the maple syrup and flax. Fold in the blueberries and top with milk, cream or vanilla yogurt (if using). Serve immediately.

Serves 4–6.

Serves 1.

Hot Cranberry Date Cereal

Shake off the chill of cooler mornings with this filling and satisfying hot cereal.

1 cup (250 mL) quinoa
2½ cups (625 mL) water
⅔ cup (160 mL) dried cranberries
¼ cup (60 mL) chopped dates or prunes
1¼ tsp (6 mL) ground flax
1 tsp (5 mL) ground cinnamon
Pinch ground nutmeg
1 tsp (5 mL) pure vanilla extract

Combine the quinoa and water in a large saucepan and bring to a boil. Add the cranberries, dates, flax, cinnamon and nutmeg. Cover and reduce to a simmer. Cook for about 17 minutes, until the quinoa is tender. Remove from the heat and stir in the vanilla. Serve with brown sugar and milk, rice milk or yogurt, if desired.

Maple Walnut Cereal

Who says you can't have it all? With the highest level of omega-3 fats compared to any other nut, walnuts are another superfood that make this classic combination a smart start to your day.

2 Tbsp (30 mL) chopped walnuts
⅓ cup (80 mL) quinoa
⅔ cup (160 mL) water
1 Tbsp (15 mL) oat bran
2 tsp (10 mL) maple syrup
Milk, vanilla yogurt or cream (optional)

Place the walnuts in a small saucepan on medium-high heat. Stir frequently until the walnuts are toasted and fragrant (about 3 to 4 minutes). Remove the pan from the heat and let the walnuts cool slightly. Chop and set aside.

Combine the quinoa, water and oat bran in a medium saucepan. Cover and bring to a boil. Reduce to a simmer and cook for 12 minutes. Leave the saucepan on the burner, covered, for an additional 6 minutes. Remove from the heat and stir in the walnuts and maple syrup. Transfer to a bowl and top with milk, yogurt or cream (if using).

Serves 4–6.

Serves 1.

Raisin Pudding Breakfast Porridge

A healthier version of the popular rice pudding, this dish makes you feel like you're eating dessert for breakfast! You can actually serve this as a dessert by increasing the sweetness to your taste.

2½ cups (625 mL) 2% milk
1 cup (250 mL) quinoa
¼ cup (60 mL) raisins
2 Tbsp (30 mL) maple syrup or honey
¼ tsp (1 mL) ground cinnamon
2 large eggs
½ tsp (2 mL) pure vanilla extract
1 Tbsp (15 mL) butter

Combine the milk, quinoa, raisins, maple syrup and cinnamon in a medium saucepan.

Cover the saucepan and bring to a boil, then reduce to a simmer and continue cooking, stirring occasionally, until the quinoa is tender, about 5 minutes.

Beat the eggs and vanilla in a small bowl. Temper the eggs by whisking in 1 tsp (5 mL) of the cooked quinoa. Repeat 7 times, whisking between each addition.

Stir the egg mixture into the saucepan. Continue to cook on low heat until the mixture thickens, about 3 to 5 minutes.

Stir in the butter and remove from the heat. Serve immediately.

Raisin Spice Cereal

With raisins, cinnamon and brown sugar, this recipe is a healthy spin on an old favorite.

1 Tbsp (15 mL) sliced almonds
⅔ cup (160 mL) water
3 Tbsp (45 mL) quinoa
1 Tbsp (15 mL) raisins
¼ tsp (1 mL) ground cinnamon
Pinch ground nutmeg
2 Tbsp (30 mL) quick-cooking rolled oats
2 tsp (10 mL) brown sugar or maple syrup
¼ cup (60 mL) milk, soy milk, half and half cream or vanilla yogurt (optional)

Toast the almonds in a small saucepan over medium-high heat, stirring frequently until fragrant, about 3 to 4 minutes. Remove the almonds and set aside.

Combine the water, quinoa, raisins, cinnamon and nutmeg in the same small saucepan and bring the mixture to a boil. Cover, reduce to a simmer and cook for 10 minutes. Stir in the oats, replace the cover and cook for an additional 6 minutes. Add the almonds and sugar. Top with milk, soy milk, cream or vanilla yogurt (if using). Serve immediately.

Serves 2.

Serves 1.

Quick Peaches-*and*-Cream Breakfast Cereal

In place of peaches, use any of your favorite fruits for this quick and easy morning blast of nutrition. Adjust the amount of honey to your desired sweetness.

½ cup (125 mL) quinoa flakes
1 cup (250 mL) milk or soy milk
2 tsp (10 mL) honey or maple syrup
½ tsp (2 mL) ground cinnamon
½ tsp (2 mL) pure vanilla extract
½ cup (125 mL) diced fresh peaches (or canned)

Combine the quinoa flakes, milk, honey and cinnamon in a medium saucepan. Cook uncovered over medium heat, stirring frequently. The quinoa flakes will cook in about 2 minutes. Remove from the heat and stir in the vanilla; add the peaches. Serve immediately.

Super Fiber Cereal

Not your average fiber cereal, this delicious breakfast is packed with so much flavor you won't even notice it's full of fiber! Using a variety of quinoa colors will add to this already bold cereal.

1 Tbsp (15 mL) sliced or chopped almonds
¼ cup (60 mL) quinoa, any color
½ cup (125 mL) water
1 Tbsp (15 mL) oat bran
½ cup (125 mL) fresh raspberries (or frozen and thawed)
2 tsp (10 mL) maple syrup
Yogurt or milk (optional)

Toast the almonds in a small saucepan on medium heat until fragrant, about 4 minutes, stirring frequently. Remove the almonds and set aside.

Combine the quinoa, water and oat bran in the same saucepan and bring to a boil. Reduce the heat, cover and simmer for 10 minutes. Turn the heat off and leave the covered saucepan on the burner for an additional 6 minutes. Stir in the raspberries, almonds and maple syrup. Serve topped with yogurt or milk (if using).

Serves 2.

Serves 4–6.

Overnight Quinoa Cereal

Make this hearty breakfast the night before and wake up to a nutritious bowl of quinoa and oats along with your favorite combination of dried or fresh fruit. Sleep late? Ready to go, it makes a healthy and light lunch or midmorning snack.

½ cup (125 mL) large-flake rolled oats
¼ cup (60 mL) quinoa flour
1 Tbsp (15 mL) brown sugar
¼ tsp (1 mL) ground cinnamon
1 cup (250 mL) plain yogurt
¼ tsp (1 mL) pure vanilla extract
¼ cup (60 mL) chopped almonds
¼ cup (60 mL) chopped dried apricots
¼ cup (60 mL) pumpkin seeds
¼ cup (60 mL) dried cranberries
1 banana (optional)

In a medium bowl, combine the oats, flour, sugar and cinnamon. Stir in the yogurt and vanilla, mixing thoroughly. Add the almonds, apricots, pumpkin seeds and cranberries and mix well. Cover and place in the refrigerator overnight.

Spoon the cereal into serving bowls. Slice the banana on top (if using). Serve cold. Stays fresh refrigerated in a sealed container for up to 2 days.

Piña Colada Quinoa

Reminiscent of a tropical holiday, this breakfast cereal also makes a nice lunch or afternoon snack. Serve it hot or cold.

1 cup (250 mL) quinoa
One 14 oz (398 mL) can light coconut milk
One 14 oz (398 mL) can crushed pineapple
1 Tbsp (15 mL) brown sugar
1 tsp (5 mL) pure vanilla extract

In a medium saucepan, bring the quinoa and coconut milk to a boil. Cover, reduce the heat to low and cook for 10 minutes. Turn off the heat and leave the covered saucepan on the burner for an additional 6 minutes.

Drain the pineapple, reserving the juice. Stir ½ cup (125 mL) of the juice into the saucepan. Add the sugar and vanilla and mix well. Stir the crushed pineapple into the mixture and serve. Store in the refrigerator in a sealed container for up to 2 days.

Makes 7 cups (1.75 L).

The Ultimate Granola

The ultimate combination of fruit, nuts and quinoa makes this granola balanced and complete. Serve with milk, soy milk or yogurt. It also makes a great snack for hiking or having at your desk at the office for those midafternoon munchies.

2½ cups (625 mL) large-flake
    rolled oats
¾ cup (185 mL) whole almonds
½ cup (125 mL) pumpkin seeds
½ cup (125 mL) sunflower seeds,
    unsalted
¼ cup (60 mL) sesame seeds
⅓ cup (80 mL) quinoa (uncooked)

¼ cup (60 mL) flaked
    unsweetened coconut
¼ cup (60 mL) walnut pieces
1 cup (250 mL) maple syrup
1 tsp (5 mL) pure vanilla extract
2 tsp (10 mL) ground cinnamon
⅓ cup (80 mL) dried cranberries
¼ cup (60 mL) raisins

Measure the oats, almonds, pumpkin seeds, sunflower seeds, sesame seeds, quinoa, coconut and walnuts into a large bowl. Mix well.

Combine the maple syrup and vanilla in a separate small bowl. Add the syrup mixture to the oat mixture and stir until evenly distributed. Sprinkle the cinnamon evenly on top of the mixture and blend well.

Spread the granola evenly on a large baking sheet and bake at 225°F (105°C) for 1 hour.

Remove and set aside to cool. Toss in the cranberries and raisins. Store the granola in a sealed container in your pantry for up to 4 weeks.

Serves 4.

Waffles

These moist, nutty-tasting waffles can be frozen for instant meals. If you don't have a waffle iron, you can make them as pancakes. Serve with your favorite toppings, such as yogurt, maple syrup, fruit syrup, peanut butter, sliced bananas, pineapple, berries or other fresh fruit, chilled coconut milk, chocolate syrup or caramel sauce.

2¼ cups (560 mL) quinoa flour
4 tsp (20 mL) baking powder
1½ Tbsp (22.5 mL) white or cane sugar
¾ tsp (4 mL) salt

2 large eggs, beaten
1¼ cups (310 mL) 1% or 2% milk
1 cup (250 mL) water
½ cup (125 mL) vegetable oil
1 tsp (5 mL) pure vanilla extract

Combine the quinoa flour, baking powder, sugar and salt in a large bowl and set aside. In a medium bowl, beat the eggs, milk, water, oil and vanilla. Add the egg mixture to the flour mixture, mixing well to make a thin batter.

Grease or lightly spray a waffle iron with cooking oil and preheat it. Pour the batter onto the waffle iron according to the manufacturer's instructions and close. Remove the waffles when the lid lifts open easily, about 5 to 6 minutes. Waffles will keep in the refrigerator for up to 3 days and sealed in a container in the freezer for up to 4 weeks. Reheat in a toaster or microwave oven.

Variation These waffles make an unusual and great-tasting sandwich! One option is shaved Black Forest ham and Monterey Jack cheese, but there are unlimited sandwich possibilities.

Serves 4.

Chocolate Quinoa Crepes *with* Bananas

A decadent morning dish full of nutrition. Topped with bananas (and a bit of chocolate sauce if you want to indulge), these light chocolate crepes are not as sinful as they appear.

⅓ cup (80 mL) quinoa flour

2 Tbsp (30 mL) unsweetened
   cocoa powder

1 Tbsp (15 mL) white sugar

Pinch salt

2 egg whites

⅓ cup (80 mL) 1% or 2% milk

¼ cup (60 mL) water

⅔ cup (160 mL) plain yogurt

2 Tbsp (30 mL) brown sugar

½ tsp (2 mL) pure vanilla extract

4 bananas, sliced

Chocolate sauce (optional)

Combine the quinoa flour, cocoa, white sugar and salt in a medium bowl, mixing well. Whisk in the egg whites, mixing gently. Slowly add the milk and water, blending until smooth. Lightly grease or spray a small frying pan with cooking oil and place over medium heat. When the pan is hot, pour about 2 Tbsp (30 mL) of the crepe batter into the pan, spreading evenly to coat. Fry until the edges begin to turn golden brown and flip, cooking about 30 seconds per side. Set aside on a plate. Repeat until all the crepes are done (you will have about 8 crepes).

In a separate bowl, combine the yogurt, brown sugar and vanilla to make the filling. Spread about 3 Tbsp (45 mL) of the filling onto each crepe. Add some sliced bananas. Wrap the crepe gently by folding in each side. Garnish the top of each crepe with additional sliced bananas and drizzle with chocolate sauce (if using). Serve immediately.

Pumpkin Pancakes

Sweet pumpkin and delicate autumn spices make this recipe enjoyable any day of the year or a special treat for any occasion. Makes about 17 pancakes.

1½ cups (375 mL) quinoa flour
¼ cup (60 mL) packed brown
   sugar
2 tsp (10 mL) baking powder
1 tsp (5 mL) baking soda
1 tsp (5 mL) ground allspice
1 tsp (5 mL) ground cinnamon
½ tsp (2 mL) ground ginger
½ tsp (2 mL) salt

1¾ cups (435 mL) buttermilk or
   sour milk
1 cup (250 mL) pumpkin purée
2 large eggs
2 Tbsp (30 mL) vegetable oil
Maple syrup
½ cup (125 mL) toasted pecans
Whipped cream (optional)

Measure the flour, sugar, baking powder, baking soda, allspice, cinnamon, ginger and salt into a large bowl. Mix well.

Whisk together the milk, pumpkin, eggs and oil in a medium bowl. Add to the flour mixture and stir until just blended.

Grease a large nonstick frying pan or spray with cooking oil and place on medium heat. When hot, pour ¼-cup (60 mL) portions of batter into the pan. Pancakes will be ready to flip when you begin to observe bubbles and the underside is brown. Flip and cook the pancake for another 20 to 25 seconds, until the center springs back when pressed. If the pancakes buckle when sliding the spatula under them, lightly oil the pan again for the next pancakes. Serve with maple syrup, pecans and whipped cream (if using).

Note If you don't have buttermilk on hand, you can use sour milk. Make it by adding 1 Tbsp (15 mL) vinegar or lemon juice to 1 cup (250 mL) milk.

Quinoa Pancakes

A traditional breakfast you can tailor to your liking. Experiment with a mixture of quinoa flour, whole wheat flour and all-purpose flour to adjust this recipe to your taste.

2⅔ cups (660 mL) quinoa flour
¼ cup (60 mL) white or cane sugar
2 Tbsp (30 mL) baking powder
  (gluten-free)
1 tsp (5 mL) salt

2½ cups (625 mL) milk or soy milk
2 large eggs
2 Tbsp (30 mL) vegetable oil
½ tsp (2 mL) pure vanilla extract

Combine the flour, sugar, baking powder and salt in a large bowl.

In a separate, medium bowl, whisk together the milk, eggs, oil and vanilla. Add to the flour mixture and whisk together until smooth.

Lightly grease a nonstick frying pan or spray with cooking oil and place on medium-high heat. When the pan is hot, pour the batter into the pan in about 4-inch (10 cm) rounds. A ¼-cup (60 mL) measure works well. When several bubbles have formed, flip the pancakes and cook for about 30 seconds, until you can gently press down in the center and it springs back. If the pancakes buckle when placing the spatula under them, the pan needs to be lightly oiled again for the next pancakes. (Note: Pancakes will be fluffier if they're only flipped once.)

Variation To make Blueberry Flax Pancakes, add ¼ cup (60 mL) of ground flax with the dry ingredients. Reduce the heat slightly to a medium setting to accommodate a slightly longer cooking time. Sprinkle with a few blueberries immediately after pouring the batter into the pan.

Makes 9.

Golden Hash Browns

Sure to be a hit at breakfast, these golden hash browns are enhanced with nutritious quinoa. Serve them with ketchup or topped with salsa, sour cream and melted cheddar cheese.

²⁄₃ cup (160 mL) water
¹⁄₃ cup (80 mL) quinoa
1½ cups (375 mL) peeled and
  grated raw potato

1 large egg
1 tsp (5 mL) salt
1 Tbsp (15 mL) butter

Bring the water and quinoa to a boil in a medium saucepan. Cover and reduce to a simmer for 10 minutes. Turn the heat off and leave on the burner, covered, for another 6 minutes. Fluff with a fork and allow the quinoa to cool.

Mix the cooked quinoa with the potato, egg and salt.

Preheat a large nonstick skillet over medium heat and melt 1 tsp (5 mL) of the butter. Working in batches, use a ¹⁄₃-cup (80 mL) measure to scoop the potato mixture into the hot skillet. Use a spatula to flatten the mixture to ½-inch (1 cm) thickness. Cook the patties for 5 minutes on each side, until golden brown. Cook the remaining mixture, adding 1 tsp (5 mL) of butter to the pan prior to each batch. Garnish as desired and serve immediately.

Jalapeño Cheddar Pepper Scramble

A quick kick of flavor, this one-pan scramble is perfect for days when you just need something different, but don't have much time. This fast and tasty recipe is great served with hot buttered toast.

½ cup (125 mL) water
¼ cup (60 mL) quinoa
1 Tbsp (15 mL) butter
½ cup (125 mL) diced red bell pepper
4 large eggs
1 Tbsp (15 mL) milk
1–2 tsp (5–10 mL) minced pickled jalapeño
    pepper
Pinch salt
¼ cup (60 mL) shredded cheddar cheese
¼ cup (60 mL) thinly sliced green onion

Bring the water and quinoa to a boil in a small saucepan. Reduce to a simmer, cover and cook for 10 minutes. Turn the heat off and leave the covered saucepan on the burner for an additional 5 minutes. Remove the lid and fluff with a fork. Set aside.

Melt the butter in a large nonstick frying pan on medium-high heat. Sauté the red pepper for about 5 to 7 minutes, until tender.

Whisk the eggs, ½ cup (125 mL) cooked quinoa, milk, jalapeño and salt in a medium bowl. Pour into the pan and cook for 3 to 4 minutes, stirring frequently to scramble the eggs. Turn the heat off and leave on the warm burner. Divide the mixture into 2 portions in the pan. Sprinkle with the cheese and green onion and allow the residual heat to melt the cheese. Serve immediately.

Light *and* Fluffy Eggs

Quinoa lightens scrambled eggs, making them even more fluffy. Dress up this dish with classic egg accompaniments, such as red, yellow or green peppers, onions, cheese, ham, sausage or mushrooms, to satisfy your morning hunger.

¼ cup (60 mL) water
2 Tbsp (30 mL) quinoa
2 large eggs
1 Tbsp (15 mL) milk
Pinch salt

Fantastic fillings (optional)
Spanish onion, green onion, mushrooms, green
    pepper, red pepper, yellow pepper, ham,
    sausage, cheddar cheese

Bring the water and quinoa to a boil in a small saucepan. Reduce to a simmer, cover and cook for 10 minutes. Turn the heat off and leave the covered saucepan on the burner for an additional 5 minutes. Remove the lid and fluff with a fork. Set aside.

Lightly grease a large nonstick skillet or spray with cooking oil and place over medium heat. Sauté or fry any vegetables or meats (if using) that you would like on a medium-high setting.

Crack the eggs into a medium bowl and whisk with the milk. Whisk the quinoa into the egg mixture. Pour the egg mixture into the hot skillet. Stir occasionally until the eggs are scrambled and cooked to your liking.

Season with salt to taste. Sprinkle with cheese if desired. Remove from the pan and serve immediately.

Serves 4.

Quinoa Breakfast Burritos

Use medium or hot salsa to give this delicious breakfast alternative an extra kick. To make it gluten-free, use brown rice tortillas.

⅔ cup (160 mL) water
⅓ cup (80 mL) quinoa
2 tsp (10 mL) butter
½ cup (125 mL) sliced white button
    mushrooms
3 green onions, sliced
4 large eggs
1 Tbsp (15 mL) milk

¼ cup (60 mL) prepared salsa
Pinch salt
4 soft whole wheat flour tortillas
    (10 or 12 inches/25 or 30 cm)
½ cup (125 mL) shredded aged
    cheddar cheese
½ cup (125 mL) light sour cream
    (optional)

Bring the water and quinoa to a boil in a small saucepan. Reduce to a simmer and cover for 10 minutes. Turn the heat off and keep the covered saucepan on the burner for an additional 5 minutes. Remove the lid and fluff with a fork. Set aside.

Preheat the oven to 225°F (105°C).

Melt the butter in a large nonstick frying pan over medium heat and sauté the mushrooms for 4 minutes. Add the sliced onions and quinoa. Continue to sauté for 2 minutes more, until the ingredients are evenly heated.

In a separate bowl, combine the eggs, milk, salsa and salt. Pour the egg mixture into the frying pan and cook, stirring frequently, until the eggs are set and no longer wet, about 3 to 4 minutes.

Place the tortillas on a baking sheet and bake on the center rack of the oven for about 4 minutes. Place a tortilla on each plate and divide the egg mixture evenly among them. Top with the cheddar cheese and a dollop of sour cream (if using). Fold 1 side of the burrito over the filling, followed by the bottom and opposite side. Serve immediately.

Ranch House Omelet

This protein-packed omelet is so full of vegetables you can enjoy it as a breakfast, lunch or dinner.

¼ cup (60 mL) water

2 Tbsp (30 mL) quinoa

1½ tsp (7.5 mL) butter

2 asparagus spears cut into 2-inch (5 cm) pieces

¼ cup (60 mL) diced white button mushrooms

2 Tbsp (30 mL) thinly sliced green onion

2 Tbsp (30 mL) halved cherry tomatoes

2 large eggs

1 Tbsp (15 mL) milk

2 tsp (10 mL) basil pesto

¼ cup (60 mL) cottage cheese (2%)

Bring the water and quinoa to a boil in a small saucepan. Reduce to a simmer, cover and cook for 10 minutes. Turn the heat off and leave the covered saucepan on the burner for an additional 5 minutes. Remove the lid and fluff with a fork. Set aside.

Melt 1 tsp (5 mL) of the butter in a nonstick frying pan on medium heat. Sauté the asparagus and mushrooms for 4 minutes. Add the green onion and sauté for another 3 minutes, or until the asparagus is tender. Remove the vegetables from the pan, mix in the tomatoes and set aside.

Heat the frying pan over medium heat and add the remaining ½ tsp (2 mL) of butter (or grease or spray with cooking oil). Whisk together the eggs, ¼ cup (60 mL) cooked quinoa, milk and pesto. Pour the mixture into the saucepan and cover with a lid or foil. Cook for about 1½ to 2 minutes, until the top of the egg is firm. Place the vegetables on one-half of the omelet. Cover and cook for 30 seconds to heat the vegetables. Transfer the omelet to a plate and spoon the cottage cheese over the vegetables. Fold the omelet in half over the filling and serve immediately.

Strawberry Shake

Rich in vitamin C, potassium and antioxidants, the wholesome combination of strawberries and quinoa provides extra nutrition for your day. If you don't have vanilla yogurt on hand, simply substitute plain or natural yogurt mixed with ¼ tsp (1 mL) pure vanilla extract and 1 tsp (5 mL) honey.

1 Tbsp (15 mL) quinoa flour
2 Tbsp (30 mL) boiling water
¾ cup (185 mL) frozen strawberries
½ cup (125 mL) vanilla yogurt
¼ cup (60 mL) milk or soy milk

Place the quinoa flour and boiling water in a small bowl. Stir until a paste has formed. Place the quinoa paste, strawberries, yogurt and milk in a blender. Purée into a smoothie and serve immediately.

Blueberry Vanilla Smoothie

If you haven't got vanilla yogurt on hand, simply mix ¼ tsp (1 mL) pure vanilla extract and 1 tsp (5 mL) honey with ¼ cup (60 mL) plain yogurt.

1 Tbsp (15 mL) quinoa flour
2 Tbsp (30 mL) boiling water
¼ cup (60 mL) milk or soy milk
¼ cup (60 mL) vanilla yogurt
1 cup (250 mL) frozen blueberries

Place the quinoa flour and boiling water in a small bowl. Stir until a paste has formed. Place the quinoa paste, milk, yogurt and frozen blueberries in a blender and purée. Serve immediately.

Serves 1.

Serves 6–8.

Tropical Beach Smoothie

A perfect blend of tropical flavors, this refreshing smoothie is sure to boost any mood. If you haven't got vanilla yogurt on hand, substitute plain or natural yogurt mixed with ¼ tsp (1 mL) pure vanilla extract and 1 tsp (5 mL) honey. Be ready to make these anytime by freezing your favorite chopped fruit in individual servings.

1 Tbsp (15 mL) quinoa flour
2 Tbsp (30 mL) boiling water
⅔ cup (160 mL) chopped pineapple
¼ cup (60 mL) frozen banana chunks
½ cup (125 mL) chopped mango
½ cup (125 mL) vanilla yogurt
1 Tbsp (15 mL) light coconut milk (optional)

Place the quinoa flour and boiling water in a small bowl. Stir until a paste has formed. Purée the quinoa paste, pineapple, banana, mango, yogurt and coconut milk (if using) in a blender. Serve immediately.

Tropical Fruit Salad

Fruit salad can be eaten at brunch, as a breakfast to go, as an accompaniment to a sandwich or as a healthy and satisfying dessert option. Top each bowl of fruit salad with a spoonful of vanilla yogurt to complete this tasty treat.

1⅓ cups (330 mL) water
⅔ cup (160 mL) white or golden quinoa
One 14 oz (398 mL) can pineapple chunks or
    tidbits, juice reserved
2–3 kiwis, peeled and chopped
1 mango, diced
Vanilla yogurt

Bring the water and quinoa to a boil in a small saucepan. Reduce to a simmer, cover and cook for 10 minutes. Turn the heat off and leave the covered saucepan on the burner for an additional 4 minutes. Fluff with a fork and set aside to cool.

Stir the cooked quinoa and pineapple juice in a large bowl until the quinoa is completely coated in juice. Gently fold in the pineapple chunks, kiwi and mango. Garnish with yogurt and serve immediately.

Refrigerate in a covered container for up to 3 days, adding the yogurt just before serving.

Breakfast Fruit *and* Oatmeal Bars

Keep these wholesome breakfast bars handy for mornings when you just don't have time to sit and eat breakfast. Easy to grab as you run out the door, these bars are packed with energy, fiber and nutrition—and they taste great.

⅓ cup (80 mL) slivered almonds
½ cup (125 mL) butter, softened
½ cup (125 mL) packed brown
    sugar
2 Tbsp (30 mL) fresh orange juice
1 Tbsp (15 mL) grated orange zest
1 tsp (5 mL) pure vanilla extract
2 large eggs
¾ cup (185 mL) unsweetened
    applesauce
½ cup (125 mL) quinoa flour

½ cup (125 mL) whole wheat flour
1 tsp (5 mL) baking powder
1 tsp (5 mL) baking soda
¼ tsp (1 mL) salt
2½ cups (625 mL) large-flake
    rolled oats
1 cup (250 mL) flaked
    unsweetened coconut
⅓ cup (80 mL) diced dried
    apricots
½ cup (125 mL) dried cranberries

Preheat the oven to 350°F (180°C). Spread the almonds evenly on a baking sheet and toast on the center oven rack for about 10 to 15 minutes, until fragrant and lightly toasted.

In a large bowl, cream the butter and sugar. Add the orange juice, orange zest, vanilla and eggs. Blend well and then stir in the applesauce.

In a separate, medium bowl, combine the quinoa and whole wheat flours, baking powder, baking soda and salt. Add this mixture to the applesauce and mix well. Stir in the almonds, oats, coconut, apricots and cranberries. Ensure the mixture is well blended, using a large wooden spoon or your hands. Chill the mixture in the freezer for 30 minutes.

With lightly greased hands, form the dough into 1- × 2-inch (2.5 × 5 cm) bars or balls and place on a large baking sheet. If you have an ice cream scoop handy, use it to scoop rounds of dough onto the baking sheet, pressing each one down with a fork to flatten it slightly.

Bake on the center oven rack for 12 to 14 minutes, until the edges are slightly golden brown. Cool on the sheet for 5 minutes before moving to a rack to cool completely. Store them for up to 2 weeks in a sealed container in the refrigerator or freeze for up to 1 month.

Chapter 2

EVERYDAY STAPLES

Appetizers, Sides, Snacks & Salads

Cooking with quinoa doesn't mean you have to sacrifice your favorite everyday foods. You may be surprised at how delicious, wholesome and fun to make these recipes are. Lively appetizers such as hummus and tabbouleh are a perfect start to a meal, and you can also impress your guests with a variety of salads, meatballs and even quesadillas—all made with quinoa to give them a healthy boost.

Black Bean Nacho Dip

An appetizer that's great for entertaining or for simple snacking.

½ cup (125 mL) water
¼ cup (60 mL) quinoa
1 cup (250 mL) cooked black beans
One 8 oz (250 g) package light cream
    cheese, softened
2 Tbsp (30 mL) milk
2 Tbsp (30 mL) fresh lime juice
3 Tbsp (45 mL) chopped fresh cilantro
¾ tsp (4 mL) ground coriander
¼ tsp (1 mL) ground cumin
Salt and ground black pepper to taste
Pinch cayenne pepper (optional)

Bring the water and quinoa to a boil in a small saucepan. Reduce to a simmer, cover and cook for 10 minutes. Turn the heat off and leave the covered saucepan on the burner for an additional 5 minutes. Remove the lid and fluff with a fork. Set aside.

Purée the black beans, cream cheese, milk and lime juice together in a blender or food processor. Blend in ½ cup (125 mL) of cooked quinoa and the cilantro, coriander, cumin, salt, black pepper and cayenne pepper (if using).

Serve with corn tortillas or toasted pita triangles. Store leftovers for up to 3 days in the refrigerator.

Quinoa Bean Dip

Served with tortilla chips, this dip is a perfect companion to the Sunday afternoon football game. Quick to whip up and high in protein and fiber, this bean dip has a tasty kick you can make as hot as you like.

½ cup (125 mL) water
¼ cup (60 mL) quinoa
One 14 oz (398 mL) can pinto beans, drained and
    rinsed
⅓ cup (80 mL) prepared salsa, hot or medium
¼ tsp (1 mL) prepared hot sauce
2 Tbsp (30 mL) chopped fresh cilantro
¼ tsp (1 mL) chili powder
¼ tsp (1 mL) ground cumin
¼ tsp (1 mL) paprika
Pinch each garlic powder, onion powder, ground
    black pepper and cayenne pepper

Bring the water and quinoa to a boil in a small saucepan. Reduce the heat to a simmer, cover and cook for 10 minutes. Turn off the heat and leave the covered saucepan on the burner for an additional 5 minutes. Remove the lid and fluff with a fork. Set aside to cool.

In a food processor or blender, purée the ½ cup (125 mL) cooked quinoa with the remaining ingredients to a smooth consistency. Store in a sealed container in the refrigerator for up to 24 hours.

Makes 2 cups (500 mL).

Makes 2½ cups (625 mL).

Quinoa Guacam-Óle!

This guacamole is thick and smooth, but if you prefer a chunkier dip, lightly mash or dice the avocado instead. Avocado has a myriad of health benefits, but it tastes so good you'll forget it is healthy.

¼ cup (60 mL) water
2 Tbsp (30 mL) quinoa
1 large ripe avocado
1 Tbsp (15 mL) fresh lime juice
1 Tbsp (15 mL) chopped onion
1 tsp (5 mL) chopped fresh cilantro
½ tsp (2 mL) minced fresh garlic
¼ tsp (1 mL) salt

Bring the water and quinoa to a boil in a small saucepan. Reduce to a simmer, cover and cook for 10 minutes. Turn the heat off and leave the covered saucepan on the burner for an additional 5 minutes. Remove the lid, fluff with a fork and set aside to cool.

Purée all the ingredients in a blender or food processor. Place the dip in a serving dish and accompany with nachos or toasted pita chips. Refrigerate for up to 2 days. To maintain color, store with plastic wrap directly on the surface of the dip.

Quinoa Hummus

An even healthier version of the popular appetizer dip served with pita bread, chips or vegetables. Not just for entertaining, it makes a tasty addition to your lunch box.

½ cup (125 mL) water
¼ cup (60 mL) quinoa
One 19 oz (540 mL) can chickpeas, drained and
  rinsed
¼ cup (60 mL) water
¼ cup (60 mL) fresh lemon juice
  (about 1–2 lemons)
2 Tbsp (30 mL) tahini
1 tsp (5 mL) minced fresh garlic
½ tsp (2 mL) ground cumin
¼ tsp (1 mL) salt
¼ tsp (1 mL) cayenne pepper (optional)
1 tsp (5 mL) minced fresh parsley (optional)

Bring the ½ cup (125 mL) water and quinoa to a boil in a small saucepan. Reduce to a simmer, cover and cook for 10 minutes. Turn the heat off and leave the covered saucepan on the burner for an additional 5 minutes. Remove the lid, fluff with a fork and set aside to cool.

Combine the chickpeas, ½ cup (125 mL) cooked quinoa, ¼ cup (60 mL) water, lemon juice, tahini, garlic, cumin, salt and cayenne pepper (if using) in a food processor or blender. Purée until smooth. Place in a serving bowl and garnish with parsley (if using). Serve with vegetables, crackers or pita wedges. Refrigerate leftovers for up to 2 days.

Quinoa Tabbouleh

Quinoa gives traditional tabbouleh a twist. Wrap this refreshing mixture in romaine lettuce leaves or serve it as a salad or North American–style as a dip with fresh pita or pita chips. Serves 6 to 8 as lettuce wraps or up to 16 when served as a dip.

1 cup (250 mL) water
½ cup (125 mL) quinoa
2 cups (500 mL) seeded and diced
  ripe tomatoes
1 cup (250 mL) diced cucumber
1 cup (250 mL) finely chopped
  fresh parsley
¼ cup (60 mL) finely chopped
  fresh mint

¼ cup (60 mL) thinly sliced green
  onion
⅓ cup (80 mL) olive oil
⅓ cup (80 mL) fresh lemon juice
  (about 1–2 lemons)
½ tsp (2 mL) salt
½ tsp (2 mL) minced fresh garlic
¼ tsp (1 mL) ground cinnamon

Bring the water and quinoa to a boil in a medium saucepan. Cover, reduce to a simmer and cook for 10 minutes. Turn the heat off and leave the covered saucepan on the burner for another 4 minutes. Fluff with a fork and allow the quinoa to cool.

Mix the tomatoes, cucumber, parsley, mint, onion and quinoa together in a large bowl.

Combine the oil, lemon juice, salt, garlic and cinnamon in a small bowl. Mix well and add to the tomato and cucumber mixture. For the best flavor, let the salad sit for 30 minutes at room temperature before serving. Refrigerate leftovers for up to 3 days.

Makes 2 cups (500 mL).

Cheese Ball

Colorful quinoa makes this a stunning and healthy appetizer. With only a few simple ingredients, this savory dish is very quick to prepare. For an alternative to green olives, use ¼ cup (60 mL) capers and ¼ cup (60 mL) toasted walnuts.

¼ cup (60 mL) red or black quinoa
½ cup (125 mL) water
One 8 oz (250 g) package light
    cream cheese, softened
2 Tbsp (30 mL) light mayonnaise
1½ tsp (7.5 mL) fresh lemon juice

1½ cups (375 mL) shredded
    reduced-fat, aged cheddar
    cheese
¼ cup (60 mL) grated onion
½ cup (125 mL) chopped green
    olives

Place the quinoa in a small saucepan over medium-high heat. Stirring frequently, lightly toast the quinoa until it is slightly fragrant, about 3 to 5 minutes. Add the water to the saucepan and bring to a boil. Cover, reduce to a simmer and cook for 10 minutes. Remove the saucepan from the heat and remove the cover. Drain any remaining liquid and allow to cool.

Combine the cream cheese, mayonnaise, lemon juice, cheese, onion, olives and half of the cooked quinoa in a large bowl. Blend the mixture with your hands and form into a large ball.

Roll the cheese ball in the remaining quinoa. (Place the cheese ball in the freezer for 15 to 20 minutes if you find it is too soft to roll in the quinoa.)

Place the cheese ball on a serving plate and serve with crackers. Refrigerate leftovers for up to 3 days.

Makes 3 cups (750 mL).

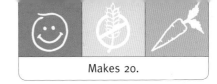

Makes 20.

Easy Cheesy Sauce

Much healthier without the thickeners of wheat flour, butter or fat used in a traditional roux, this sauce is gluten-free, fast and foolproof. This cheese sauce will become the only one you ever use!

2 cups (500 mL) milk
⅓ cup (80 mL) quinoa flour
½ tsp (2 mL) salt
½ tsp (2 mL) Dijon mustard (or ¼ tsp/1 mL mustard powder)
¼ tsp (1 mL) ground black pepper
1½ cups (375 mL) shredded aged cheddar cheese

Whisk together the milk, flour, salt, mustard and pepper in a medium saucepan over medium heat. Whisk frequently until the sauce thickens and covers the back of a spoon, about 5 to 7 minutes. Remove from the heat and whisk in the cheddar cheese.

Use in all of your favorite cheesy dishes such as pastas and casseroles, or serve with steamed vegetables.

Stuffed Mushrooms

This version of an old favorite is lower in fat and packed with quinoa goodness. This recipe looks good using red or black quinoa.

3 Tbsp (45 mL) quinoa
6 Tbsp (90 mL) water
20 white button mushrooms
¼ cup (60 mL) butter
¼ cup (60 mL) minced onion
¼ cup (60 mL) finely chopped pistachios
3 Tbsp (45 mL) finely chopped fresh parsley
¼ tsp (1 mL) dried oregano
¼ cup (60 mL) freshly grated Parmesan cheese

Preheat the oven to 400°F (200°C).

Bring the quinoa and water to a boil in a small saucepan. Cover, reduce to a simmer and cook for 10 minutes. Turn the heat off and leave the covered saucepan on the burner for another 4 minutes. Fluff with a fork and allow the quinoa to cool.

Gently twist the mushroom stems to remove them. Finely dice the stems. Melt the butter in a small saucepan and sauté the stems and onion on medium-low heat until the onion is opaque and tender, 3 to 4 minutes. Remove from the heat and allow to cool.

Stir the quinoa, pistachios, parsley and oregano into the butter, mushroom and onion mixture. Using a teaspoon, scoop the filling into the mushroom caps and place them on a baking sheet. Bake for 12 minutes, until the mushrooms are tender. Sprinkle with Parmesan cheese and serve warm.

Santa Fe Meatballs

Not your average meatball, this modern version is an instant hit for any gathering. Great for finger food or served on a sandwich. To keep this gluten-free, make sure you use gluten-free bacon.

½ cup (125 mL) water
¼ cup (60 mL) quinoa
1 lb (500 g) lean ground beef or turkey
6 slices bacon, finely chopped and cooked
½ cup (125 mL) finely chopped onion
¼ cup (60 mL) finely chopped fresh cilantro, Italian parsley or curly parsley

2 large eggs
1 Tbsp (15 mL) minced fresh garlic
2 tsp (10 mL) minced pickled jalapeños
1 tsp (5 mL) ground cumin
½ tsp (2 mL) salt
1 lime

Bring the water and quinoa to a boil in a small saucepan. Reduce to a simmer, cover and cook for 10 minutes. Turn the heat off and leave the covered saucepan on the burner for an additional 5 minutes. Remove the lid and fluff with a fork. Set aside.

Preheat the oven to 400°F (200°C).

Combine the ground meat, ½ cup (125 mL) cooked quinoa, bacon, onion, cilantro, eggs, garlic, jalapeños, cumin and salt in a medium bowl. Blend well and form the mixture into 1-inch (2.5 cm) meatballs. Place them on a large nonstick baking sheet or one lined with parchment paper. Bake for about 7 to 8 minutes, then turn the meatballs and cook for another 7 to 8 minutes, until they are no longer pink inside. Juice the lime and drizzle over the meatballs. Serve immediately.

Serves 4–6.

Black Bean Quinoa Quesadillas

This versatile dish works well as a side, a complete meal or even finger food during the football game. Add grilled chicken or beef for an even heartier dish. Use brown rice tortillas to make this recipe gluten-free.

½ cup (125 mL) water
¼ cup (60 mL) quinoa
½ cup (125 mL) cooked black
    beans
¼ cup (60 mL) finely diced fresh
    tomatoes
¼ cup (60 mL) corn kernels
¼ cup (60 mL) thinly sliced green
    onion

1 Tbsp (15 mL) minced fresh
    cilantro
8 soft whole wheat tortillas
    (8 inches/20 cm) (or brown
    rice tortillas)
¾ cup (185 mL) shredded aged
    cheddar cheese

Bring the water and quinoa to a boil in a small saucepan. Reduce to a simmer, cover and cook for 10 minutes. Turn the heat off and leave the covered saucepan on the burner for an additional 5 minutes. Remove the lid and fluff with a fork. Set aside.

Preheat the oven to 375°F (190°C). Combine the ½ cup (125 mL) of cooked quinoa and black beans in a medium bowl. Lightly mash the mixture with a potato masher to bind it together. Add the tomatoes, corn, green onion and cilantro and mix thoroughly.

Place 4 of the tortillas on 1 large or 2 small baking sheets.

Spread the mixture evenly over the tortillas. Sprinkle evenly with the cheese and cover with the remaining 4 tortillas.

Place on the middle rack of the oven and bake for 12 minutes, until the cheese is melted and the filling is heated through. The edges of the quesadillas should be lightly browned.

Remove from the oven and cut into triangles. Serve with fresh guacamole, salsa and sour cream.

Serves 4–6.

Cauliflower *and* Broccoli Bake *with* Toasted Almonds

Cauliflower and broccoli are closely related, and both are high in fiber and rich in phytonutrients and vitamin C. This dish is also loaded with potassium, calcium and vitamin A, just to name a few. All this and delicious, too!

3 cups (750 mL) cauliflower florets
3 cups (750 mL) broccoli florets
2 cups (500 mL) milk
¼ cup (60 mL) quinoa flour
1 tsp (5 mL) prepared mustard
½ tsp (2 mL) minced fresh garlic
½ tsp (2 mL) salt
¼ tsp (1 mL) ground black pepper
Pinch ground nutmeg
1 cup (250 mL) shredded aged
   cheddar cheese
1 cup (250 mL) sliced raw almonds

Ensure you move the top oven rack to accommodate a 9- × 13-inch (3.5 L) casserole dish, with a second rack underneath to toast the almonds.

Preheat the oven to 350°F (180°C) and grease a 9- × 13-inch (3.5 L) casserole dish or spray with cooking oil.

Steam the cauliflower and broccoli together in a large saucepan until just barely tender. Place them in the bottom of the baking dish.

Combine the milk, quinoa flour, mustard, garlic, salt, pepper and nutmeg in a medium saucepan over low heat. Simmer, whisking the mixture until the flour is well blended. Add the cheese as the mixture begins to thicken. Continue cooking and whisking until the cheese is melted and the mixture is smooth and coats the back of a spoon. Pour the sauce over the vegetables. Bake the casserole uncovered in the oven for 20 minutes, until hot and bubbly.

After the casserole has baked for 13 minutes, place the sliced almonds on a small baking sheet on the bottom rack of the oven, under the casserole. Toast the almonds for 7 minutes, until fragrant and lightly toasted. Remove both the casserole and the toasted almonds from the oven, sprinkle the almonds generously on top of the casserole and serve immediately.

Mushroom *and* Herb Quinoa

The bold color and flavor of this recipe make it a great side for a pork, chicken or beef dish. If you can't find cremini mushrooms, use an extra cup (250 mL) of button mushrooms.

1 Tbsp (15 mL) butter or cooking oil
⅓ cup (80 mL) sliced green onion
½ tsp (2 mL) minced fresh garlic
¾ cup (185 mL) red quinoa
1¾ cups (435 mL) vegetable stock
1 cup (250 mL) quartered white button mushrooms
1 cup (250 mL) quartered brown cremini mushrooms
Pinch ground black pepper
2 Tbsp (30 mL) minced fresh parsley
⅔ cup (160 mL) freshly grated Parmesan cheese

Heat the butter in a large saucepan, add the green onion and garlic and cook on low for about 5 minutes, stirring frequently. Add the quinoa and stir to coat it with butter.

Add the vegetable stock and bring to a boil. Reduce the heat and simmer uncovered for about 20 minutes, or until most of the stock has been absorbed, stirring frequently.

Add the mushrooms and cook for another 15 minutes, stirring frequently, until the liquid has been completely absorbed.

Add a pinch of pepper and stir in the parsley and grated Parmesan cheese. Serve immediately.

Mushroom Broccoli Quisotto

Similar to a traditional risotto, this quick-to-prepare side dish is healthy but definitely not short on flavor. Substitute asparagus for the broccoli if you prefer.

2 Tbsp (30 mL) butter
2 cups (500 mL) chopped broccoli, cut into
  2-inch (5 cm) pieces
2 cups (500 mL) chopped white button
  mushrooms
½ cup (125 mL) diced white onion
1 Tbsp (15 mL) minced fresh garlic
1 cup (250 mL) quinoa
2 cups (500 mL) vegetable or chicken stock
Pinch ground nutmeg
¼ cup (60 mL) chopped fresh parsley
⅓ cup (80 mL) freshly grated Parmesan cheese
Salt and pepper to taste

Melt the butter in a large saucepan. Sauté the broccoli, mushrooms, onion and garlic until tender, about 10 minutes, stirring frequently.

Combine the quinoa, stock and nutmeg in a medium saucepan and bring to a boil. Reduce to a simmer, cover and cook until the quinoa is completely tender, about 10 minutes. Leave the covered saucepan on the burner for 6 minutes to allow residual heat in the pot to complete the cooking.

Add the cooked quinoa to the broccoli and mushrooms. Gently stir in the parsley, Parmesan cheese, salt and pepper. Serve immediately.

Savory Stuffing

This healthy version of stuffing can be used in place of all your seasonal stuffing recipes or as a poultry side dish. For the gluten-free version, ensure you use gluten-free bacon.

2 Tbsp (30 mL) butter
1 cup (250 mL) diced onion
1 cup (250 mL) diced celery
1 cup (250 mL) chopped white button
  mushrooms
¾ cup (185 mL) quinoa
1½ cups (375 mL) chicken broth
1 bay leaf
1 tsp (5 mL) poultry seasoning
¼ tsp (1 mL) dried marjoram
1 Tbsp (15 mL) chopped fresh parsley
¼ cup (60 mL) crumbled cooked bacon (optional)
Salt and pepper to taste

Melt the butter in a medium saucepan and sauté the onion, celery and mushrooms for about 7 minutes or until tender. Add the quinoa, broth, bay leaf, poultry seasoning and marjoram. Cover, reduce to a simmer and cook for 10 minutes. Turn off the heat and leave the covered saucepan on the burner for 7 more minutes. Toss in the parsley and bacon (if using). Season with salt and pepper.

Asian Sprout Salad

Chock full of vegetables and sprouts, this salad can conveniently be prepared the night before. It will keep in a sealed container in the refrigerator for up to four days, but wait until serving time to add the nuts.

¼ cup (60 mL) slivered almonds
1 cup (250 mL) quinoa sprouts (page 56)
1 cup (250 mL) thinly sliced purple cabbage,
   cut in 1-inch-long (2.5 cm) pieces
1 cup (250 mL) grated carrots
1 cup (250 mL) diced red bell pepper (about
   1 pepper)
1 cup (250 mL) halved fresh stringless snap peas
¼ cup (60 mL) sliced green onion
2 Tbsp (30 mL) sesame oil
2 Tbsp (30 mL) rice vinegar
2 Tbsp (30 mL) soy sauce (or gluten-free tamari)
2 Tbsp (30 mL) honey

Preheat the oven to 350°F (180°C). Spread the almonds evenly on a baking sheet and bake on the center oven rack for 5 to 7 minutes, until the almonds are fragrant and lightly toasted. Remove from the oven and set aside.

Combine the sprouts, cabbage, carrots, red pepper, peas and onion in a large bowl.

Whisk together the oil, vinegar, soy sauce and honey and set them aside.

Toss the almonds and dressing with the vegetables and serve.

Cucumber Mint Salad

The flavor of fresh mint in this crisp salad makes it a great partner to any summer meal.

1½ cups (375 mL) water
¾ cup (185 mL) quinoa
1 long English cucumber, seeded and diced
½ cup (125 mL) finely chopped red onion
¼ cup (60 mL) chopped fresh parsley
¼ cup (60 mL) chopped fresh mint
1 tsp (5 mL) minced fresh garlic
3 Tbsp (45 mL) fresh lemon juice
¼ cup (60 mL) olive oil
1 Tbsp (15 mL) apple cider vinegar
¼ tsp (1 mL) salt
Pinch ground black pepper

Bring the water and quinoa to a boil in a small saucepan. Reduce to a simmer, cover and cook for 10 minutes. Turn the heat off and leave the covered saucepan on the burner for an additional 4 minutes. Remove the lid and fluff with a fork. Set aside to cool.

Combine the cooked quinoa, cucumber, onion, parsley and mint in a medium bowl.

Whisk the garlic, lemon juice, olive oil, vinegar, salt and pepper in a small bowl. Pour the vinegar mixture over the vegetable mixture and toss until well combined. Serve immediately.

Bocconcini *and* Oregano Salad

The delicate flavor of this popular Italian cheese and the crisp vegetables blend perfectly with the oregano vinaigrette.

¾ cup (185 mL) quinoa

1½ cups (375 mL) water

1 cup (250 mL) diced zucchini

1 cup (250 mL) halved cherry tomatoes

½ cup (125 mL) diced red onion

½ cup (125 mL) frozen baby green peas, thawed

1 cup (250 mL) diced red bell pepper (about 1 pepper)

½ cup (125 mL) diced yellow bell pepper

3 Tbsp (45 mL) balsamic vinegar

2 Tbsp (30 mL) extra virgin olive oil

1 Tbsp (15 mL) Dijon mustard

2 Tbsp (30 mL) finely chopped fresh oregano (or 2 tsp/10 mL dried oregano)

1 tsp (5 mL) minced fresh garlic

Pinch salt

Pinch ground black pepper

1 cup (250 mL) halved mini bocconcini cheese pieces

Bring the quinoa and water to a boil in a medium saucepan. Cover, reduce to a simmer and cook for 10 minutes. Turn the heat off and leave the covered saucepan on the burner for another 4 minutes. Remove the lid and fluff the cooked quinoa with a fork. Set aside to completely cool.

Combine the zucchini, tomatoes, onion, peas and red and yellow pepper in a large bowl.

Whisk the vinegar, olive oil, mustard, oregano, garlic, salt and pepper together in a small bowl. Pour the dressing over the vegetables and thoroughly mix all the ingredients. Add the quinoa and bocconcini and mix until evenly combined. Serve immediately or refrigerate for up to 3 days.

Fresh Cucumber *and* Toasted Almond Salad *with* Dill

Toasted quinoa and almonds nicely complement this crisp salad of cucumber, green onion and fresh dill.

½ cup (125 mL) sliced raw almonds
1 cup (250 mL) quinoa
2 cups (500 mL) vegetable or
   chicken stock
3 Tbsp (45 mL) extra virgin olive oil
3 Tbsp (45 mL) white wine vinegar
   or white rice vinegar

½ tsp (2 mL) salt
2 cups (500 mL) chopped English
   cucumber
½ cup (125 mL) sliced green onion
¼ cup (60 mL) chopped fresh dill

Preheat the oven to 350°F (180°C). Spread the almonds evenly on a baking sheet and bake on the center oven rack for 5 to 7 minutes, until the almonds are fragrant and lightly toasted. Remove from the oven and set aside.

Place the quinoa in a large saucepan over medium heat. Toast the quinoa for 3 to 5 minutes, until it is fragrant but not browned, shaking the saucepan from side to side occasionally to turn the quinoa and toast it evenly. (Note: If you use a saucepan with a larger bottom it will toast faster.)

Add the stock to the saucepan and bring to a boil. Reduce the heat to low and cover. Simmer for 10 minutes, then turn the heat off and leave the covered saucepan on the burner for an additional 4 minutes. Remove the lid, fluff the quinoa with a fork and transfer to a large bowl to cool completely.

Whisk together the oil, vinegar and salt in a small bowl. Add to the cooled quinoa and mix thoroughly. Add the cucumber, green onion and dill, tossing well. Just before serving, sprinkle with the toasted almonds.

Best if enjoyed immediately but can be refrigerated in a sealed container for up to 3 days.

Dill Potato Salad

Sprouted quinoa makes this potato salad a fresh alternative to the traditional recipe. Stored in a sealed container in the refrigerator, it will stay fresh for up to three days. If you prefer the creamier version and don't mind the extra calories, use mayonnaise instead of yogurt.

4 large potatoes, peeled and diced
½ cup (125 mL) high-fat plain yogurt (10%)
1½ tsp (7.5 mL) fresh lemon juice
2 Tbsp (30 mL) chopped fresh dill
1 green onion, thinly sliced
¾ cup (185 mL) quinoa sprouts (page 56)

Boil the potatoes for 10 to 12 minutes, until tender. Drain and set them aside to cool.

In a medium bowl, mix together the yogurt, lemon juice, dill and green onion. Gently fold in the quinoa sprouts and potatoes. Mix well. Chill for about 1 hour. Garnish with additional sprigs of dill and serve.

Mandarin Almond Salad

As good as any salad you would find in a deli, this is a perfect accompaniment to pork or chicken entrées. It also packs well for lunches.

1¾ cups (435 mL) water
½ cup (125 mL) brown lentils
½ cup (125 mL) quinoa
¼ cup (60 mL) canola oil
4 tsp (20 mL) apple cider vinegar
1 Tbsp (15 mL) fresh lime juice
3 Tbsp (45 mL) canned mandarin orange juice
¼ tsp (1 mL) salt
½ cup (125 mL) slivered almonds
½ cup (125 mL) dried cranberries
3 Tbsp (45 mL) minced fresh parsley
One 10 oz (284 mL) can mandarin orange segments, drained (juice reserved)

Place the water in a large saucepan over high heat and bring to a boil. Rinse the lentils in cold water and add them to the boiling water. Cover, lower to a simmer and cook for 18 minutes.

Add the quinoa to the lentils and return to a boil, then reduce the temperature to a simmer and cook for 10 minutes.

Turn off the heat and let the covered saucepan sit on the burner for 4 minutes. Drain any remaining water. Remove the lid and fluff with a fork. Set aside to cool.

Whisk together the oil, vinegar, lime juice, mandarin juice and salt to make the dressing. Combine the dressing with the lentil and quinoa mixture. Stir in the almonds, cranberries and parsley. Add the mandarin orange segments and toss gently. Serve.

Pomegranate, Almond *and* Feta Salad

Great for entertaining, this eye-catching salad has an intense flavor combination of feta, toasted almonds and pomegranate. The addition of spinach and quinoa makes for a super wholesome dish. This looks fantastic when made with black quinoa, but use red or white if you prefer. Serves four as a small meal or six as a side salad.

½ cup (125 mL) water
¼ cup (60 mL) black quinoa
½ cup (125 mL) sliced almonds
4 cups (1 L) baby spinach leaves
¾ cup (185 mL) crumbled light
   feta
¼ cup (60 mL) sliced red onion

1 pomegranate, seeded
3 Tbsp (45 mL) red wine vinegar
3 Tbsp (45 mL) olive oil
4 tsp (20 mL) honey
1 tsp (5 mL) Dijon mustard
Salt and pepper to taste

Bring the water and quinoa to a boil in a small saucepan. Reduce to a simmer, cover and cook for 10 minutes. Turn the heat off and leave the covered saucepan on the burner for an additional 4 minutes. Remove the lid and fluff with a fork. Set aside to cool.

Preheat the oven to 350°F (180°C). Spread the almonds on a baking sheet and toast in the oven for about 5 to 7 minutes, until they are fragrant and lightly browned.

Divide the spinach into 4 large or 6 small servings. Sprinkle the feta, onion, quinoa, pomegranate seeds and toasted almonds evenly over the salads.

Whisk the vinegar, oil, honey and Dijon in a small bowl. Season with salt and pepper. Drizzle the dressing over the salads and serve.

Quinoa Bean Salad

This salad is similar to a regular bean salad, with the added nutrition of cooked or sprouted quinoa.

1 cup (250 mL) water

½ cup (125 mL) quinoa

One 19 oz (540 mL) can chickpeas, drained and rinsed

One 14 oz (398 mL) can kidney beans, drained and rinsed

1 cup (250 mL) sliced green bell pepper

1 cup (250 mL) diced celery

¾ cup (185 mL) chopped red onion

½ cup (125 mL) apple cider vinegar

¼ cup (60 mL) olive oil

2 tsp (10 mL) minced fresh garlic

2 tsp (10 mL) dried oregano

½ tsp (2 mL) ground black pepper

Bring the water and quinoa to a boil in a medium saucepan. Cover, reduce to a simmer and cook for 10 minutes. Turn the heat off and leave the covered saucepan on the burner for another 4 minutes. Fluff with a fork and allow the quinoa to cool.

Combine the quinoa, chickpeas, kidney beans, green pepper, celery and onion in a large bowl.

In a small bowl mix the vinegar, oil, garlic, oregano and black pepper until well blended.

Add the dressing to the salad, mix well and serve immediately.

Variation Replace cooked quinoa with 1½ cups (375 mL) of quinoa sprouts (page 56).

Quinoa Chickpea Salad

This salad is a perfect complement to almost any main course, especially summer barbecues. It also makes a great lunch to go. Protein-rich chickpeas, also called garbanzo beans, have plenty of fiber and are thought to lower cholesterol and help balance blood sugar levels.

2 cups (500 mL) vegetable stock

1 cup (250 mL) quinoa

One 19 oz (540 mL) can chickpeas, drained and rinsed

1 cup (250 mL) diced red bell pepper (about 1 pepper)

⅓ cup (80 mL) dried cranberries

⅓ cup (80 mL) chopped walnuts

3 Tbsp (45 mL) chopped fresh parsley

Bring the stock and quinoa to a boil in a medium saucepan over high heat. Reduce to a simmer, cover and cook for 10 minutes. Turn the heat off and leave the covered saucepan on the burner for 4 more minutes. Fluff with a fork and allow the quinoa to cool.

Transfer the quinoa to a large bowl and mix in the chickpeas, red pepper, cranberries, walnuts and parsley. Chill before serving. Stays fresh in a sealed container in the refrigerator for up to 5 days.

Serves 4–6.

Pimento *and* Chickpea Quinoa

The fusion of lemon, capers and pimento will make this filling salad a regular favorite.

½ cup (125 mL) quinoa

1 cup (250 mL) water

Two 19 oz (540 mL) cans chickpeas, drained and rinsed

⅓ cup (80 mL) finely chopped fresh parsley

One 2 fl oz (57 mL) jar sliced pimentos, drained

3 Tbsp (45 mL) capers, drained

2 Tbsp (30 mL) sliced green onion

2 Tbsp (30 mL) olive oil

2 Tbsp (30 mL) fresh lemon juice

2 tsp (10 mL) Dijon mustard

½ tsp (2 mL) minced fresh garlic

Pinch cayenne pepper

Bring the quinoa and water to a boil in a small saucepan. Reduce to a simmer, cover and cook for 10 minutes. Turn the heat off and leave the covered saucepan on the burner for an additional 4 minutes. Remove the lid, fluff with a fork and allow the quinoa to cool.

Combine the chickpeas, parsley, pimentos, capers, green onion and quinoa in a large bowl and set aside.

In a separate bowl, mix the oil, lemon juice, mustard, garlic and cayenne until well blended. Pour the dressing over the chickpea and quinoa mixture and stir well. For the best flavor, let the salad sit at room temperature for 30 minutes prior to serving.

Serves 4–6.

Serves 4–6.

Southwest Quinoa Salad

A classic southwestern blend of black beans, corn and cilantro.

2 cups (500 mL) water
1 cup (250 mL) quinoa
⅓ cup (80 mL) olive oil
⅓ cup (80 mL) fresh lime juice (about 2–3 limes)
4 tsp (20 mL) apple cider vinegar
2½ tsp (12 mL) ground cumin
1 tsp (5 mL) finely minced jalapeño, Fresno or
    Mirasol pepper (optional)
1¼ cups (310 mL) frozen corn kernels, thawed
1 cup (250 mL) diced red bell pepper
    (about 1 pepper)
One 14 oz (398 mL) can black beans, drained
    and rinsed
⅓ cup (80 mL) chopped fresh cilantro
¼ tsp (1 mL) salt

Bring the water and quinoa to a boil in a medium saucepan. Cover, reduce to a simmer and cook for 10 minutes. Turn the heat off and leave the covered saucepan on the burner for another 4 minutes. Fluff with a fork and allow the quinoa to cool.

Place the quinoa in a large bowl. Whisk the oil, lime juice, apple cider vinegar, cumin and jalapeño (if using) in a small bowl. Stir the dressing into the quinoa. Toss with the corn, red pepper, black beans, cilantro and salt. Serve immediately or cover and refrigerate in a sealed container for up to 3 days.

Sunny Summer Salad

Perfect for summer gatherings, this salad can be prepared the night before to take along to a family picnic, a barbecue or the cottage.

1½ cups (375 mL) water
¾ cup (185 mL) quinoa
2 cups (500 mL) finely diced zucchini
1 cup (250 mL) finely diced red bell pepper
    (about 1 pepper)
1 cup (250 mL) finely diced yellow bell pepper
⅓ cup (80 mL) sunflower seeds, roasted and
    unsalted
⅓ cup (80 mL) dried currants
2 Tbsp (30 mL) minced fresh parsley
2 Tbsp (30 mL) minced fresh cilantro
⅓ cup (80 mL) fresh lemon juice
    (about 1–2 lemons)
¼ cup (60 mL) olive oil
1 tsp (5 mL) minced fresh garlic
½ tsp (2 mL) salt
Pinch each cayenne pepper, ground cumin and
    ground turmeric

Bring the water and quinoa to a boil in a small saucepan. Reduce to a simmer, cover and cook for 10 minutes. Turn the heat off but keep the covered saucepan on the burner for an additional 4 minutes. Remove the lid, fluff with a fork and allow to cool.

Place the zucchini, red and yellow peppers, sunflower seeds, currants, parsley and cilantro in a large bowl. Add the cooled quinoa. Whisk the lemon juice, oil, garlic, salt, cayenne, cumin and turmeric in a small bowl. Pour the dressing over the salad ingredients and gently toss until evenly distributed.

Sushi Salad

This salad has all the elements to please any sushi lover. It makes a light lunch or would be a great addition to a dinner party menu.

1½ cups (375 mL) water
¾ cup (185 mL) quinoa
1 Tbsp (15 mL) fish sauce
1 Tbsp (15 mL) soy sauce
1 Tbsp (15 mL) white or cane sugar
½ tsp (2 mL) red pepper flakes
¼ tsp (1 mL) cayenne pepper
½ tsp (2 mL) minced fresh garlic
1½ cups (375 mL) imitation crabmeat
1 cup (250 mL) cored and diced English cucumber
   (unpeeled)
5 green onions, chopped
1 tsp (5 mL) finely chopped pickled ginger
1 tsp (5 mL) black sesame seeds (optional)

Bring the water and quinoa to a boil in a medium saucepan. Cover, reduce to a simmer and cook for 10 minutes. Turn the heat off and leave the covered saucepan on the burner for another 4 minutes. Fluff with a fork and allow the quinoa to cool.

Whisk the fish sauce, soy sauce, sugar, pepper flakes, cayenne and garlic in a large bowl. Add the quinoa and toss.

Cut the crabmeat into 1-inch (2.5 cm) pieces. Add the crabmeat, cucumber, green onions and ginger to the quinoa and gently toss. Garnish with black sesame seeds (if using). Serve.

Tomato Quinoa Salad

A zesty salad with a touch of heat.

½ cup (125 mL) quinoa
1 cup (250 mL) water
¼ cup (60 mL) fresh lemon juice
   (about 1–2 lemons)
2 Tbsp (30 mL) tomato paste
2 Tbsp (30 mL) olive oil
1 tsp (5 mL) finely minced pickled jalapeño
   pepper
¼ tsp (1 mL) chili powder
¼ tsp (1 mL) salt
2 cups (500 mL) diced tomato
¼ cup (60 mL) finely chopped fresh parsley
¼ cup (60 mL) finely chopped fresh mint
⅓ cup (80 mL) thinly sliced green onion

Bring the quinoa and water to a boil in a medium saucepan. Cover, reduce to a simmer and cook for 10 minutes. Turn the heat off and leave the covered saucepan on the burner for another 4 minutes. Fluff with a fork and allow the quinoa to cool.

In a small bowl blend the lemon juice, tomato paste, oil, jalapeño, chili powder and salt and mix well. In a separate bowl, combine the quinoa, tomato, parsley, mint and onion. Add the dressing to the quinoa mixture just before serving.

Quinoa Sprouts

*Sprouted quinoa has concentrated amounts of vita-
mins and minerals. It is a great addition to salads,
sandwiches and sides or can just be munched as
a snack for that extra boost of living enzymes! The
quantity of sprouts you get will depend on the duration of the sprouting process.*

2/3 cup (160 mL) quinoa
2 cups (500 mL) distilled cold water

Place the quinoa and water in a 10-inch (25 cm)
round or square covered casserole dish or
glass bowl. Ensure all the seeds are completely
immersed in water, cover and soak them for
40 minutes at room temperature.

Drain the quinoa and rinse thoroughly with
water. Return the quinoa to the original dish
and replace the cover, but leave a slight opening
for air. Cover completely with a kitchen towel.
Let the sprouts rest for 8 to 10 hours. Repeat
the rinse-and-rest process 1 to 2 more times
depending on how long you like your sprouts.
The shorter the sprouts, the longer they last in
the refrigerator. Be sure to use longer sprouts
quickly, preferably within 24 hours.

Garlic Toasted Quinoa

*Use this crunchy, savory topping in place of croutons
on any of your favorite salads.*

1 Tbsp (15 mL) butter
¼ tsp (1 mL) garlic salt
½ cup (125 mL) quinoa

Preheat the oven to 350°F (180°C). Melt the butter
in a small frying pan on medium heat and add
the garlic salt. Remove from the heat and add
the quinoa, tossing lightly to coat with butter.

Spread the quinoa on a large baking sheet.
Bake for 10 to 12 minutes, until the quinoa is
toasted and fragrant. Remove from the oven
and cool. Use immediately or store in a sealed
container in the refrigerator for 6 to 8 weeks.

Chapter 3

EVERYDAY SOUPS & STEWS

Healthful & Hearty

Quinoa dramatically improves the quality and nutritional impact of everyday soups and stews. These incredible recipes may have you forgetting it's even in there. Warm your home with comforting, hearty soups and stews made with fresh ingredients in recipes such as Curried Carrot Soup and Buffalo Quinoa Potage as well as traditional favorites like Italian Wedding Soup.

Serves 4–6.

Black Bean Soup

This spicy Mexican-inspired soup is enlivened with the fresh flavors of lime and cilantro.

1 Tbsp (15 mL) olive oil
½ cup (125 mL) chopped onion
½ cup (125 mL) quinoa
2 cups (500 mL) chicken or
  vegetable broth
Two 19 oz (540 mL) cans black
  beans, drained and rinsed
1 tsp (5 mL) finely minced fresh
  garlic
1 tsp (5 mL) chili powder
½ tsp (2 mL) ground cumin

¼ tsp (1 mL) red pepper flakes
2 Tbsp (30 mL) chopped fresh
  cilantro
1 Tbsp (15 mL) fresh lime juice
¼ tsp (1 mL) salt
½ cup (125 mL) tortilla chips
½ cup (125 mL) shredded aged
  cheddar cheese
½ cup (125 mL) plain yogurt or
  sour cream (optional)

Place the olive oil in a large saucepan over medium-high heat. Add the onion and sauté for 5 to 6 minutes. Add the quinoa and toast until lightly fragrant, about 4 minutes.

Add the broth, black beans and garlic to the saucepan and bring to a boil. Cover and reduce to a simmer. Cook until the quinoa is tender, stirring frequently for about 14 minutes.

Add the chili powder, cumin and red pepper flakes. Purée the cooked mixture with a hand blender or cool slightly and purée in 2 batches in a blender or food processor. Return the soup to the saucepan over low heat. Stir in the cilantro, lime juice and salt. Ladle into wide bowls and top with tortilla chips, cheddar cheese and plain yogurt or sour cream (if using).

Beef Vegetable Quinoa Soup

The blend of herbs in this traditional beef vegetable soup takes this recipe from ordinary to extraordinary.

1 Tbsp (15 mL) cooking oil	1 bay leaf
1 cup (250 mL) diced stewing beef	3 sprigs fresh parsley
½ cup (125 mL) diced onion	½ cup (125 mL) diced red bell
½ cup (125 mL) diced carrots	pepper
½ cup (125 mL) diced celery	¼ cup (60 mL) green peas (frozen
¼ cup (60 mL) quinoa	or fresh)
4 cups (1 L) beef broth	Salt and ground black pepper to
1 sprig fresh rosemary	taste
1 sprig fresh thyme	

Heat the oil in a large saucepan on medium-high heat. Place the beef in the pan and brown for about 5 minutes. Add the onion, carrots and celery. Cook until the onion is opaque, about 10 minutes. Add the quinoa and beef broth.

Make a bouquet garni (bundle of herbs) by placing the rosemary, thyme, bay leaf and parsley in a small 4-inch (10 cm) square piece of cheesecloth and tying it with a cotton string. (You can also simply tie the herbs together with a string.) Immerse the bundle in the soup.

Simmer the soup for about 17 minutes, until the quinoa is tender. Add the red pepper and peas in the last 8 minutes of cooking. Remove the fresh herbs, season with salt and pepper and serve.

Serves 4–6.

Broccoli Cheese Soup

This recipe is sure to be your newest family favorite! For a completely different flavor, try ¾ cup (185 mL) of blue cheese instead of the cheddar.

3 cups (750 mL) broccoli florets
1 Tbsp (15 mL) butter
1 cup (250 mL) chopped onion
¼ cup (60 mL) quinoa
3 cups (750 mL) chicken or
    vegetable stock

1½ cups (375 mL) half and half
    cream (10–12%)
Salt and ground black pepper to
    taste
1 cup (250 mL) shredded aged
    cheddar cheese

Separate the broccoli into smaller, bite-sized pieces and set aside. Melt the butter in a large saucepan over medium heat. Add the onion and sauté until softened, about 8 to 10 minutes. Add the broccoli, quinoa and chicken stock to the saucepan. Cover and reduce the heat to low. Simmer for about 18 minutes, until the quinoa is tender.

Purée the cooked mixture with a hand blender or cool slightly and purée in 2 batches in a blender or food processor. Return the soup to the saucepan and add the cream. Season with salt and pepper. Reheat the soup on low heat, being careful not to boil it. When the soup is hot, stir in the cheese until just melted and serve immediately.

Serves 4.

Chilled Avocado Soup

The vitamin E–rich avocado is a stroke and heart disease preventative, containing monounsaturated fat that may lower your cholesterol. It has also been suggested that this fruit promotes nutrient absorption in the body and may even be anti-aging. This fresh, chilled soup tastes great on scorching summer days when you wouldn't even consider eating hot soup. Make it look incredible by using red quinoa. This is fantastic paired with any light sandwich or wrap.

½ cup (125 mL) water
¼ cup (60 mL) quinoa
3 ripe avocados, peeled and diced
¾ cup (185 mL) diced cucumber
1 tsp (5 mL) diced onion
1 tsp (5 mL) minced fresh garlic
2 cups (500 mL) vegetable stock

1 cup (250 mL) water
⅓ cup (80 mL) prepared salsa, medium or hot
4 slices cucumber
Prepared hot sauce or red pepper sauce

Bring the water and quinoa to a boil in a small saucepan. Reduce to a simmer, cover and cook for 10 minutes. Turn the heat off and leave the covered saucepan on the burner for an additional 5 minutes. Remove the lid and fluff with a fork.

In a food processor or blender, purée the avocados, quinoa, cucumber, onion and garlic. Slowly add the vegetable stock, water and salsa to the mixture and continue to blend until smooth. Chill in a sealed container for at least 30 minutes and up to 24 hours. Pour into 4 chilled bowls and garnish each serving with a thin slice of fresh cucumber and a dash of hot sauce.

Serves 4–6.

Serves 4–6.

Curried Carrot Soup

Carrots don't have to be boring! Rich in flavor, this cost-effective soup will have you saying, "I can't believe it tastes so good."

1 cup (250 mL) chopped onion
2 cups (500 mL) peeled and diced carrots
1 cup (250 mL) peeled and diced potatoes
5 cups (1.25 L) vegetable broth
1 Tbsp (15 mL) curry powder
1 tsp (5 mL) minced fresh garlic
½ cup (125 mL) quinoa flour
⅓ cup (80 mL) coconut milk
    (or 1 cup/250 mL 2% milk)
2 Tbsp (30 mL) chopped fresh cilantro
Salt to taste

In a large saucepan, combine the onion, carrots, potato, broth, curry powder and garlic. Cover the saucepan and bring to a boil, then reduce the heat and simmer for 1 hour.

Blend in the quinoa flour. Remove from the heat and cool slightly. Purée the cooked mixture with a hand blender or in 2 batches in a blender or food processor. Any lumps will disappear with this step. Return the mixture to the saucepan and add the coconut milk, cilantro and salt. Gently reheat on a medium setting for about 5 minutes and serve.

Dill Beet Soup

The sweet taste of this thick, vibrant and iron-rich soup makes it a delightful meal all on its own. Serve with a thick slab of crusty bread. Store it in a sealed container in the refrigerator for up to four days.

1 Tbsp (15 mL) olive oil
¾ cup (185 mL) finely chopped onion
¾ cup (185 mL) quinoa
3 cups (750 mL) vegetable broth
1 cup (250 mL) water
2 large beets, peeled and chopped
1 tsp (5 mL) minced fresh garlic
¼ cup (60 mL) chopped fresh dill
¼ cup (60 mL) fresh lemon juice
    (about 1–2 lemons)
1 tsp (5 mL) salt
Pinch ground black pepper
¼ cup (60 mL) sour cream or low-fat plain yogurt

In a large saucepan, heat the olive oil over medium-high heat. Add the onion and sauté for about 4 minutes. Add the quinoa and toast until fragrant, about 2 minutes. Add the broth and water and bring to a boil. Add the beets and cook for 5 to 7 minutes. Add the garlic. Reduce the heat, cover and simmer for an additional 10 to 15 minutes, until the beets are tender. Remove from the heat.

Purée the cooked mixture with a hand blender or cool slightly and purée in 2 batches in a blender or food processor. Return the mixture to the saucepan and stir over low heat. Add the dill, lemon juice, salt and pepper. Garnish each serving with a scoop of sour cream or yogurt.

Serves 4–6.

Italian Wedding Soup

A staple offered in many restaurants. The term "wedding" refers to how well the flavors are married.

Meatballs	½ lb (250 g) extralean ground turkey 1 large egg ¼ cup (60 mL) thinly sliced green onion 3 Tbsp (45 mL) dry breadcrumbs	2 Tbsp (30 mL) chopped fresh cilantro 2 Tbsp (30 mL) freshly grated Parmesan cheese 1 Tbsp (15 mL) chopped fresh basil (or 1 tsp/5 mL dried)
Soup	6 cups (1.5 L) chicken stock ½ cup (125 mL) quinoa 2½ cups (625 mL) thinly sliced fresh spinach	2–3 tsp (10–15 mL) grated lemon zest (about 1 lemon) Freshly grated Parmesan cheese (garnish)

To make the meatballs, combine the turkey, egg, green onion, bread-crumbs, cilantro, cheese and basil in a large bowl. Mix together thoroughly and shape into ¾-inch (2 cm) meatballs.

For the soup, bring the chicken stock to a boil in a large saucepan. Add the quinoa, reduce to a simmer, cover and cook for 8 minutes.

Drop the meatballs into the boiling stock and gently stir. Bring back to a simmer, cover and cook for another 5 minutes. Stir in the spinach and lemon zest, cover and cook for an additional 5 minutes.

Serve with freshly grated Parmesan cheese on the side.

Leek *and* Potato Soup

Just a few simple ingredients, but this soup is far from bland.

3 Tbsp (45 mL) butter
2 cups (500 mL) sliced leeks, white parts only
3 cups (750 mL) chicken or vegetable broth
2½ cups (625 mL) peeled and diced Yukon gold
    potatoes
½ cup (125 mL) quinoa
2 cups (500 mL) milk or soy milk
Salt to taste

Melt the butter in a large saucepan and sauté the leeks until tender, about 8 minutes. Remove ½ cup (125 mL) of the sautéed leeks and set aside.

Add the broth, potatoes and quinoa to the saucepan and bring to a boil. Cover, reduce to a simmer and cook until the potatoes and quinoa are tender, about 18 minutes. Purée the cooked mixture with a hand blender or cool slightly and purée in 2 batches in a blender or food processor. Return the purée to the saucepan and stir in the milk and the reserved leeks. Heat on medium but do not boil. Season with salt. Remove from the heat and serve.

Lemon Quinoa Soup

Inspired by the popular Greek lemon soup, this creamy soup is a zesty midwinter pick-me-up. If you want to cut calories, skip the cream in this recipe. This soup tastes just as great without it.

1 Tbsp (15 mL) extra virgin olive oil
4 green onions, thinly sliced
½ cup (125 mL) quinoa
3 cups (750 mL) chicken or vegetable broth
3 cups (750 mL) water
4 large eggs
¼ cup (60 mL) fresh lemon juice
    (about 1–2 lemons)
Pinch ground black pepper
1 cup (250 mL) half and half cream (10–12%)
1 tsp (5 mL) grated lemon zest

In a large saucepan, heat the olive oil over medium heat. Add the green onions and sauté until tender, about 4 minutes. Add the quinoa and stir to coat. Toast for another 4 to 5 minutes, stirring occasionally. Add the broth and water and bring to a boil over medium-high heat. Reduce the heat and simmer for an additional 10 to 15 minutes, until the quinoa is tender.

In a medium bowl, whisk the eggs and lemon juice together. Temper the egg mixture by slowly whisking 1 cup (250 mL) of the hot broth into the egg. Stir the warm egg mixture into the broth. Stir in the pepper, cream and lemon zest. Simmer for a few more minutes to heat, being careful not to boil the soup. Serve immediately. This soup will keep in the refrigerator for up to 3 days.

Serves 4–6.

Light *and* Creamy Mushroom Soup

If you're a mushroom fan, you'll love this soup. Mushrooms are thought to be anti-bacterial and boost immune response.

½ cup (125 mL) quinoa
2 Tbsp (30 mL) butter
1 cup (250 mL) diced onion
8 cups (2 L) chopped white button
   mushrooms
4 cups (1 L) chicken or vegetable
   stock
1 tsp (5 mL) minced fresh (or
   roasted) garlic

1 cup (250 mL) half and half cream
   (10–12%) (more for garnish)
½ tsp (2 mL) salt
Pinch ground black pepper
3 Tbsp (45 mL) half and half cream
   (10–12%; optional)
3 Tbsp (45 mL) finely chopped
   chives (optional)

Place the quinoa in a large, dry saucepan over medium heat. Toast the quinoa until fragrant, about 5 minutes, stirring frequently. Place the quinoa in a bowl and set aside.

Melt the butter in the same large saucepan and sauté the onion and mushrooms until the onion is opaque and tender, about 7 to 8 minutes. Remove 1½ cups (375 mL) of the mixture and set aside. Add the toasted quinoa, stock and garlic to the saucepan and bring to a boil. Cover, reduce to a simmer and cook until the quinoa is tender, about 18 minutes. Purée the cooked mixture with a hand blender or cool slightly and purée in 2 batches in a blender or food processor. Return the soup to the saucepan. Season with salt and pepper. Add the reserved mushroom mixture and the 1 cup (250 mL) of cream. Reheat gently, being sure not to boil the soup. Garnish each serving with a drizzle of cream and some chives (if using).

Serves 4–6.

Minestrone Soup

This humble but hearty soup has long been an economical staple in the kitchens of Italy. This is a fresh, wholesome version of the classic.

2 Tbsp (30 mL) olive oil
1 cup (250 mL) diced white onion
1 cup (250 mL) diced carrots
1 cup (250 mL) diced potatoes
½ tsp (2 mL) salt
One 14 oz (398 mL) can diced
    tomatoes, including liquid
3 cups (750 mL) vegetable or
    chicken stock

½ cup (125 mL) quinoa
2 tsp (10 mL) minced fresh garlic
1 cup (250 mL) diced zucchini
½ cup (125 mL) freshly grated
    Parmesan cheese
1 cup (250 mL) thinly sliced fresh
    spinach
2 Tbsp (30 mL) finely chopped
    fresh parsley

Heat the oil in a large saucepan over medium heat. Sauté the onion, carrots, potatoes and salt until the onion is tender and opaque, about 7 minutes. Stir in the tomatoes and their liquid, vegetable stock, quinoa and garlic.

Cook for about 18 minutes, until the quinoa and vegetables are tender. Add the zucchini and ¼ cup (60 mL) of the Parmesan cheese and simmer for 5 additional minutes. Stir in the spinach and parsley and cook for 1 minute. Ladle the soup into bowls and garnish each with a sprinkle of the remaining Parmesan cheese.

Serves 4–6.

Mint *and* Green Pea Soup

Traditionally, pea soup has many versions across many cultures. This is a bright and simple blend of green peas and quinoa with a sweet touch of mint.

2 Tbsp (30 mL) butter or olive oil
¼ cup (60 mL) finely chopped onion
4 cups (1 L) frozen sweet peas
2 cups (500 mL) chicken or vegetable stock

⅓ cup (80 mL) quinoa flour
2 cups (500 mL) 2% milk
¼ cup (60 mL) chopped fresh mint
Pinch sugar
Salt and ground black pepper to taste

Place the butter in a large saucepan over medium heat. Add the onion and sauté until opaque, about 4 minutes. Add the peas and stock to the saucepan and simmer for 20 minutes. Remove from the heat and purée the cooked mixture with a hand blender or cool slightly and purée in 2 batches in a blender or food processor.

In a medium bowl, whisk the quinoa flour with the milk. Return the pea soup to medium heat and add the quinoa and milk mixture. Add the fresh mint.

Bring the soup to a simmer and cook for about 5 minutes, stirring frequently. Season with sugar, salt and pepper and serve.

Roasted Red Pepper Tomato Soup

The rich flavors of roasted red pepper and fresh basil will place this quick-to-prepare tomato soup at the top of your favorites list. Ready-to-use roasted red peppers are easy to find in the pickle section of the grocery store. Freeze for up to one month.

3 Tbsp (45 mL) butter
¾ cup (185 mL) chopped onion
One 28 oz (796 mL) can crushed
    tomatoes
1 cup (250 mL) diced roasted red
    pepper
¼ cup (60 mL) finely chopped
    fresh basil

2 tsp (10 mL) white or cane sugar
½ tsp (2 mL) salt
2 cups (500 mL) vegetable or
    chicken stock
½ cup (125 mL) quinoa flour
1 cup (250 mL) half and half cream
    (10–12%)

Melt the butter in a medium saucepan on medium heat. Sauté the onion until tender and opaque, about 8 minutes. Add the tomatoes, red pepper, basil, sugar and salt.

Whisk the stock and flour together in a medium bowl. Slowly stir the mixture into the saucepan (a few lumps are fine). Bring to a boil, then lower the temperature and simmer for 5 minutes.

Remove from the heat and purée the cooked mixture with a hand blender or cool slightly and purée in 2 batches in a blender or food processor.

Return the soup to the lowest heat setting. Stir in the cream and adjust the seasoning, if desired. Serve immediately.

Serves 4–6.

Quinoa, Leek *and* Corn Chowder

Quinoa makes this a lovely thick soup without the addition of heavy cream. The cayenne gives it a subtle warm flavor.

1 Tbsp (15 mL) butter
1 cup (250 mL) chopped onion
1 cup (250 mL) sliced leek (white part only)
½ cup (125 mL) quinoa
3 cups (750 mL) frozen corn kernels

2 cups (500 mL) chicken or vegetable broth
1 red bell pepper, chopped
Pinch ground black pepper
¼ tsp (1 mL) cayenne pepper
5 saffron threads
¼ tsp (1 mL) salt

In a large saucepan, melt the butter and sauté the onion and leek until the onion is tender and opaque, about 7 minutes. Add the quinoa and 2 cups (500 mL) of the corn; set aside the remaining corn to thaw. Cook for an additional 5 minutes, until the corn partially thaws. Add a few drops of the broth to keep it from sticking to the saucepan, if necessary.

Add the broth and bring to a boil. Reduce the heat, cover and simmer for 15 minutes or until the quinoa is completely cooked. Remove from the heat. Purée the cooked mixture with a hand blender or cool slightly and purée in 2 batches in a blender or food processor. Return the mixture to low heat. Add the remaining 1 cup (250 mL) of corn and the red pepper, black pepper, cayenne, saffron and salt. Reheat and stir. Serve immediately. The soup can be stored in a sealed container in the refrigerator for 2 days.

Serves 4–6.

Rustic Vegetable Soup

This country-style vegetable soup is a great way to use a bunch of ingredients from your refrigerator.

1 Tbsp (15 mL) butter
4 cups (1 L) chopped white button
    mushrooms (or a mixture of
    mushrooms)
¾ cup (185 mL) diced Spanish
    onion
¾ cup (185 mL) halved and thinly
    sliced leek (white part only)
½ cup (125 mL) diced celery
1 tsp (5 mL) minced fresh garlic

½ tsp (2 mL) salt
4 cups (1 L) vegetable or chicken
    stock
¾ cup (185 mL) diced carrots
½ cup (125 mL) diced zucchini
¼ cup (60 mL) quinoa
2 tsp (10 mL) minced fresh basil
    (or ½ tsp/2 mL dried)
Freshly ground black pepper
    (optional)

Melt the butter in a large saucepan on medium heat. Sauté the mushrooms, onion, leek, celery, garlic and salt until the vegetables have softened, about 12 minutes.

Add the stock, carrots, zucchini, quinoa and basil and bring to a boil. Reduce to a simmer, cover and cook for 20 minutes. Season with pepper (if using) and serve.

Sweet Potato *and* Coconut Quinoa Soup

The subtle hint of cayenne and chili pepper, along with the flavor of coconut, makes this soup exotic and unusual—the perfect escape. Store it in a sealed container in the refrigerator for up to two days.

2 large sweet potatoes	1 cup (250 mL) coconut milk
2 Tbsp (30 mL) water	¼ tsp (1 mL) cayenne pepper
½ cup (125 mL) diced onion	¼ tsp (1 mL) chili powder
½ cup (125 mL) quinoa	¼ cup (60 mL) plain yogurt
3 cups (750 mL) vegetable stock	(optional)

Wash and peel the sweet potatoes and cut into 2- to 3-inch (5 to 7.5 cm) pieces. Boil for 5 to 6 minutes, until just soft but not mushy.

Place the water and onion in a large saucepan over medium heat and cook until the onion softens, about 7 minutes. Stir in the quinoa and vegetable stock and bring to a boil. Reduce the heat to medium and cook for about 15 minutes, until the quinoa is cooked.

Add the sweet potato to the saucepan. Purée the mixture with a hand blender or cool slightly and purée in 2 batches in a blender or food processor. Return to low heat and stir in the coconut milk. Reheat slowly on low, adding the cayenne and chili powder. Ladle into bowls and top each serving with a spoonful of plain yogurt (if using).

Serves 4–6.

Serves 4–6.

Hearty Beans *and* Greens Stew

This tasty, one-pot stew is fast to make when you're short on time. This recipe is easily modified to be vegetarian—just use vegetable stock and omit the meat.

4 cups (1 L) chicken or vegetable stock
1 cup (250 mL) diced onion
½ cup (125 mL) quinoa
¾ tsp (4 mL) dried oregano
1 tsp (5 mL) minced fresh garlic
1 bay leaf
2 cups (500 mL) cooked red kidney beans
2 cups (500 mL) cooked navy beans
2 cups (500 mL) chopped spinach, kale or
    Swiss chard leaves
2 cups (500 mL) diced rotisserie chicken or
    diced cooked low-fat Italian sausage
Pinch ground black pepper
Salt to taste

Combine the stock, onion, quinoa, oregano, garlic and bay leaf in a large saucepan and bring to a boil. Reduce to a simmer, cover and cook for 15 minutes. Remove the lid and add the kidney beans, navy beans and spinach. Cook until the spinach has wilted. Stir in the chicken, season with salt and pepper and serve. Refrigerate leftovers for up to 2 days.

Chicken Vegetable Stew

This classic standby is thickened and nutritionally enhanced with quinoa flour. Serve with fresh biscuits or bread.

1 Tbsp (15 mL) olive oil
1 cup (250 mL) diced carrots
1 cup (250 mL) diced celery
¾ cup (185 mL) diced onion
2 cups (500 mL) chicken stock
1 cup (250 mL) halved baby red potatoes
1 tsp (5 mL) minced fresh garlic
1 bay leaf
1 Tbsp (15 mL) finely chopped fresh dill
    (or 1 tsp/5 mL dried)
2 cups (500 mL) diced cooked chicken breast
    (2–3 breasts)
1 cup (250 mL) diced red bell pepper
    (about 1 pepper)
½ cup (125 mL) quinoa flour
1 cup (250 mL) cold water
1 tsp (5 mL) salt
¼ tsp (1 mL) ground black pepper

Heat the olive oil in a large saucepan on medium-high heat. Add the carrots, celery and onion. Sauté the vegetables until they begin to soften, about 8 minutes. Stir in the chicken stock, potatoes, garlic, bay leaf and dill. Cover and bring to a boil. Reduce the heat to low and simmer for 8 minutes. Add the chicken and red pepper. Remove the bay leaf.

Whisk the flour and water together in a small bowl. Add the flour mixture to the saucepan and cook until the stew thickens, about 5 minutes, stirring occasionally. Season with salt and pepper and serve immediately.

Serves 4–6.

Quinoa, Carrot *and* Lentil Stew

The lentil is said to be one of the first domesticated crops, dating back to prehistoric times. An important component of any vegetarian diet, lentils are high in protein and often used as a meat substitute. To make this recipe a soup rather than a stew, reduce the thickness by precooking the quinoa, then adding it to the soup.

½ cup (125 mL) quinoa
½ cup (125 mL) red lentils
4 cups (1 L) vegetable or chicken
   stock
1 cup (250 mL) water
1½ cups (375 mL) sliced carrots
1 cup (250 mL) diced red onion
2 tsp (10 mL) minced fresh garlic

1 tsp (5 mL) ground cumin
1 tsp (5 mL) ground coriander
¼ tsp (1 mL) salt
1 cup (250 mL) diced red bell
   pepper (about 1 pepper)
2 Tbsp (30 mL) finely chopped
   fresh cilantro

Combine the quinoa, lentils, stock and water in a large saucepan and bring to a boil. Reduce to a simmer, cover and cook for 10 minutes. Add the carrots, onion, garlic, cumin, coriander and salt and cook for 5 minutes. Add the red pepper and cook for 5 more minutes. Add the cilantro and adjust the seasoning if necessary. Serve immediately.

Beef *and* Sweet Potato Tagine *on* Quinoa

Served on a bed of quinoa, this exotic and hearty slow-cooked Moroccan stew is a full meal that will warm even the coldest of winter days. Prepare it up to one day in advance, slowly reheat and serve.

Tagine		
1 Tbsp (15 mL) olive oil		1 tsp (5 mL) ground cumin
1 cup (250 mL) finely chopped onion		1 tsp (5 mL) ground coriander
2 tsp (10 mL) minced fresh ginger		1 tsp (5 mL) paprika
2 lb (1 kg) diced stewing beef		1 cinnamon stick
2½ cups (625 mL) canned tomatoes, with liquid		1¼ cups (310 mL) peeled and diced sweet potatoes
½ cup (125 mL) water		½ cup (125 mL) pitted, chopped dates

Quinoa		
2 cups (500 mL) vegetable stock		¼ cup (60 mL) sliced almonds, toasted (optional)
1 cup (250 mL) quinoa		

To make the tagine, preheat a large saucepan over medium heat. Add the olive oil and sauté the onion until softened and opaque, about 4 minutes. Add the ginger and beef chunks and brown the meat thoroughly. Add the tomatoes, water, cumin, coriander, paprika and cinnamon stick. Bring to a boil. Add the sweet potatoes and cook uncovered for 12 to 15 minutes, until the sweet potatoes are slightly tender. Reduce the heat and add the chopped dates to the mixture. Continue to simmer uncovered for 5 minutes.

To prepare the quinoa, bring the vegetable stock and quinoa to a boil in a medium saucepan. Cover, reduce to a simmer and cook for 10 minutes. Turn the heat off and leave the covered saucepan on the burner for another 6 minutes. Fluff with a fork and set aside.

Preheat the oven to 350°F (180°C). Spread the almonds (if using) evenly on a baking sheet and bake on the center oven rack for 5 to 7 minutes, until fragrant and lightly toasted. Remove from the oven and set aside.

To serve, spoon the quinoa onto individual serving plates and top with a large scoop of tagine. Garnish with a generous sprinkle of toasted almonds and serve.

Serves 8.

Buffalo Quinoa Potage

Buffalo is iron rich and provides more nutrients than beef, with fewer calories. It tastes similar to conventional beef but is a healthier option because buffalo graze on grass rather than living in a feedlot, so are exposed to fewer hormones and chemicals. If you can't get buffalo, substitute lean beef, preferably organic.

1 Tbsp (15 mL) cooking oil
1 lb (500 g) buffalo meat, cubed
½ cup (125 mL) chopped onion
1 tsp (5 mL) minced fresh garlic
½ cup (125 mL) quinoa
1 cup (250 mL) sliced carrots
2 Tbsp (30 mL) chopped fresh
    parsley
½ tsp (2 mL) dried thyme

4 cups (1 L) beef broth
1 cup (250 mL) water
2 cups (500 mL) diced potatoes
2 cups (500 mL) diced and peeled
    sweet potatoes
½ cup (125 mL) diced celery
½ cup (125 mL) peas (fresh or
    frozen)

Place the cooking oil and buffalo meat in a large nonstick saucepan and brown over medium heat for about 5 minutes. Add the onion, garlic and quinoa and continue to cook for 5 minutes, stirring frequently. Add the carrots, parsley, thyme and 1 to 2 Tbsp (15 to 30 mL) of beef broth to the saucepan; cook for an additional 5 minutes.

Add the remaining beef broth and the water and bring to a boil. Add the potatoes, sweet potatoes and celery. Reduce to a simmer, cover and continue cooking on low heat for 45 minutes.

In the last 10 minutes of cooking, add the peas. Ladle into bowls and serve immediately. This stew can be kept in a covered container in the refrigerator for 2 days or frozen for up to 1 month.

Chapter 4

EVERYDAY ENTRÉES

For Both Carnivores & Vegetarians!

Whether you are a meat eater or vegetarian or simply enjoy varying your menus with dishes that include less meat, these flexible and flavorful recipes, ranging from sandwiches with sprouts to chili and soufflés, will comfort and delight you. Quinoa injects additional nutrition into dishes for every occasion, from simple, light meals such as the tuna salad sandwich to impressive, substantial repasts like Peruvian Peppered Steak on Quinoa and Quinoa-Stuffed Chicken Breasts.

Chicken Broccoli Casserole

A hint of curry gives this cheesy chicken dish a subtle flavor. Even children will devour it.

1 cup (250 mL) quinoa	½ cup (125 mL) light mayonnaise
2 cups (500 mL) water	2 tsp (10 mL) fresh lemon juice
3 cups (750 mL) broccoli florets (fresh or frozen)	2 tsp (10 mL) prepared mustard
2 Tbsp (30 mL) vegetable or olive oil	1 tsp (5 mL) curry powder
4 boneless, skinless chicken breasts	½ tsp (2 mL) minced fresh basil (or a pinch dried basil)
1½ cups (375 mL) light sour cream	1 cup (250 mL) shredded cheddar cheese

Preheat the oven to 350°F (180°C). Lightly grease a 9- × 13-inch (3.5 L) casserole dish or spray with cooking oil.

Bring the quinoa and water to a boil in a medium saucepan. Cover, reduce to a simmer and cook for 10 minutes. Turn the heat off and leave the covered saucepan on the burner for another 6 minutes. Fluff with a fork and cool. Evenly spread the cooked quinoa over the bottom of the casserole. Set aside.

Cook the broccoli in a steamer or medium saucepan until just tender or al dente. Arrange the broccoli over the quinoa in the casserole dish.

Heat the oil in a large nonstick pan over medium-high heat. Brown the chicken breasts until cooked and the juices run clear, about 5 minutes on each side. Cool the chicken slightly, then slice into 2-inch-wide (5 cm) strips and place evenly over the broccoli.

Combine the sour cream, mayonnaise, lemon juice, mustard, curry powder and basil in a small bowl and mix well. Spread evenly over the chicken and top with the shredded cheese. Bake on the center oven rack for about 25 minutes, until the casserole is hot and the cheese is melted and bubbly.

Serves 4–6.

Ginger Edamame Quinoa

Get the essentials of fiber, protein, calcium, vitamin C and iron in this amazingly complete entrée loaded with superfoods.

1 cup (250 mL) quinoa
2 cups (500 mL) water
2 Tbsp (30 mL) vegetable oil
2 Tbsp (30 mL) water
2 cups (500 mL) broccoli florets
1 cup (250 mL) chopped red bell
    pepper (about 1 pepper)
½ tsp (2 mL) minced fresh garlic
½ tsp (2 mL) ground ginger (or
    1 tsp/5 mL grated fresh ginger)

2 cups (500 mL) cooked diced
    chicken, beef, pork or whole
    shrimp, or diced tofu
1 cup (250 mL) cooked black beans
1 cup (250 mL) edamame beans,
    shelled and steamed
3 Tbsp (45 mL) soy sauce or
    gluten-free tamari

Bring the quinoa and the 2 cups (500 mL) of water to a boil in a medium saucepan. Cover, reduce to a simmer and cook for 10 minutes. Turn the heat off and leave the covered saucepan on the burner for another 6 minutes. Fluff with a fork and set aside.

Heat a large wok or saucepan on medium heat. Add the oil, the 2 Tbsp (30 mL) of water and the broccoli. Cover and cook the mixture for 4 minutes. Add the red pepper, garlic and ginger, replace the cover and cook for an additional 3 minutes, until the broccoli and peppers are tender yet crisp. Add the chicken, black beans, edamame and soy sauce. Stir in the quinoa and continue to heat until it is heated throughout. Serve immediately. Refrigerate any leftovers for up to 2 days.

Serves 4–6.

Mango Chicken Quinoa

Sweet, tart mangoes make this dish exotic.

2 cups (500 mL) chicken or
   vegetable stock
1 cup (250 mL) quinoa
1 Tbsp (15 mL) olive oil
4 boneless, skinless chicken
   breasts, diced
1¼ cups (310 mL) diced zucchini
1 cup (250 mL) diced red bell
   pepper (about 1 pepper)

2 Tbsp (30 mL) orange juice
1 ripe mango, diced
2 Tbsp (30 mL) chopped fresh
   cilantro
1 cup (250 mL) shredded aged
   cheddar cheese
½ cup (125 mL) light sour cream

Bring the stock and quinoa to a boil in a medium saucepan. Cover, reduce to a simmer and cook for 10 minutes. Turn the heat off and leave the covered saucepan on the burner for another 6 minutes. Fluff with a fork and set aside.

Heat the oil in a large saucepan over medium-high heat. Add the diced chicken and cook for 5 minutes, stirring the chicken to lightly brown on all sides. Add the zucchini and red pepper and continue to cook for another 10 minutes, until the vegetables are tender and the chicken is thoroughly cooked. Add the orange juice and stir to coat all the ingredients. Continue cooking until the mixture is warm throughout. Fold in the mango and cilantro and allow to heat slightly.

To serve, place a layer of quinoa on individual serving plates and top with the mango chicken mixture. Garnish with the cheddar cheese and a dollop of sour cream. Serve immediately.

Serves 4.

Moroccan Chicken *on* Quinoa

The exotic fragrance, color and blend of flavors in this Middle Eastern dish satisfy all the senses.

Chicken	
½ tsp (2 mL) ground cinnamon	1 cup (250 mL) diced onion
¼ tsp (1 mL) ground ginger	1 cup (250 mL) water
¼ tsp (1 mL) ground turmeric	2 tsp (10 mL) minced fresh garlic
¼ tsp (1 mL) ground coriander	3 Tbsp (45 mL) orange juice
2 Tbsp (30 mL) butter or vegetable oil	Pinch salt
4 boneless, skinless chicken breasts	

Quinoa	
⅔ cup (160 mL) quinoa	½ tsp (2 mL) salt
1⅓ cups (330 mL) water	½ tsp (2 mL) ground cinnamon
1 Tbsp (15 mL) butter	⅓ cup (80 mL) pistachios
2 tsp (10 mL) honey	

To prepare the chicken, combine the cinnamon, ginger, turmeric and coriander in a small bowl and set aside. Melt the butter in a large sauce-pan on medium heat and place the chicken breasts in the pan. Fry for about 5 minutes, until they are nicely browned. Flip the chicken over and add the onion, water, garlic, orange juice and salt. Toss in the spices. Cover and bring to a boil, then reduce to a simmer and cook for about 20 to 25 minutes, until the chicken is no longer pink.

While the chicken is simmering, prepare the quinoa by bringing the quinoa and water to a boil in a small saucepan. Reduce to a simmer, cover and cook for 10 minutes. Turn the heat off and leave the covered saucepan on the burner for an additional 7 minutes. Remove the lid and fluff with a fork.

Remove the quinoa from the heat and toss with the butter, honey and salt. Stir in the cinnamon and pistachios.

To serve, divide the quinoa among 4 plates and top each with a piece of chicken. Pour the sauce overtop. Refrigerate leftovers for up to 2 days.

Serves 4.

Quinoa-Crusted Chicken *with* Sage

Fresh sage, Dijon and Gouda cheese take ordinary chicken to new heights. A side salad dressed with balsamic vinaigrette makes a great accompaniment.

Chicken	3 Tbsp (45 mL) milk	½ cup (125 mL) quinoa flakes
	3 tsp (15 mL) Dijon mustard	6 tsp (30 mL) finely chopped fresh
	½ tsp (2 mL) minced fresh garlic	sage
	¾ tsp (4 mL) Worcestershire sauce	½ tsp (2 mL) salt
	⅓ cup (80 mL) freshly grated	4 boneless, skinless chicken
	Parmesan cheese	breasts

Cheese sauce	¼ cup (60 mL) milk	Pinch each salt and ground black
	2 tsp (10 mL) quinoa flour	pepper
	¾ cup (185 mL) grated Gouda	
	cheese	

Preheat the oven to 400°F (200°C). Lightly grease a baking sheet, spray with cooking oil or line with parchment paper.

Mix the milk and 2 tsp (10 mL) of the mustard in a small, shallow bowl. Add the garlic and Worcestershire sauce and mix well. Set aside.

Combine the Parmesan, quinoa flakes, 2 tsp (10 mL) of the sage and the salt and place in a shallow bowl. Working with 1 chicken breast at a time, dip evenly into the milk mixture, then place in the bowl and coat with the quinoa mixture.

Place the chicken breasts on the baking sheet and bake on the center rack for about 20 minutes, until the meat is no longer pink and the juices run clear.

To make the sauce, heat the milk and the quinoa flour in a small saucepan on medium heat, stirring frequently. Whisk in the cheese with the remaining 4 tsp (20 mL) sage and 1 tsp (5 mL) Dijon mustard. Heat the mixture until it thickens, about 3 to 4 minutes, whisking frequently. Season the sauce with salt and pepper. Pour the sauce over the cooked chicken and serve immediately.

Quinoa-Stuffed Chicken Breasts

A lightly seasoned chicken breast is wrapped around a savory quinoa filling with melted goat cheese. Perfect with a small spinach salad.

½ cup (125 mL) water
¼ cup (60 mL) quinoa
¾ cup (185 mL) crumbled goat
    cheese
2 Tbsp (30 mL) chopped black
    olives
3 Tbsp (45 mL) diced red bell
    pepper
1 green onion, thinly sliced

¼ tsp (1 mL) ground black pepper
3 tsp (15 mL) dried oregano
1 large egg
4 large boneless, skinless chicken
    breasts
2 Tbsp (30 mL) extra virgin
    olive oil
2 Tbsp (30 mL) fresh lemon juice
¼ tsp (1 mL) salt

Preheat the oven to 400°F (200°C).

Bring the water and quinoa to a boil in a small saucepan. Reduce to a simmer, cover and cook for 10 minutes. Turn the heat off and leave the covered saucepan on the burner for an additional 6 minutes. Remove the lid and fluff with a fork.

In a small bowl, combine the quinoa, goat cheese, olives, red pepper, green onion, black pepper and 2 tsp (10 mL) of the oregano. Add the egg and blend well. Spoon the mixture onto the center of each chicken breast, roll up and secure with a toothpick. Place the rolled chicken breasts in a 9- × 13-inch (3.5 L) casserole dish.

In a separate small bowl, combine the olive oil, lemon juice, salt and remaining oregano. Drizzle the mixture over the chicken.

Bake on the center oven rack for 20 minutes. Remove from the oven and let the chicken stand for 3 to 4 minutes before serving.

Thai Cashew Chicken *and* Broccoli *on* Quinoa

Lovers of Thai food will enjoy this everyday dish: it's full of flavors inspired by Thai cuisine.

4 boneless, skinless chicken
 breasts (or 8 boneless thighs)
¼ cup (60 mL) soy sauce or
 gluten-free tamari
2 Tbsp (30 mL) oyster sauce
1 tsp (5 mL) minced fresh garlic
1 tsp (5 mL) ground ginger (or 2
 tsp/10 mL minced fresh ginger)
2 cups (500 mL) water

1 cup (250 mL) quinoa
4 tsp (20 mL) sesame oil
2 cups (500 mL) broccoli florets
1 cup (250 mL) thinly sliced onion
¾ cup (185 mL) water
3 Tbsp (45 mL) peanut butter
1 Tbsp (15 mL) honey
1 cup (250 mL) unsalted toasted
 cashews

Slice the chicken into thin pieces and place in a large, sealable plastic bag. Combine the soy sauce, oyster sauce, garlic and ginger in a bowl and pour into the bag with the sliced chicken. Place in the refrigerator for at least 1 hour (and up to 24 hours) to marinate.

Bring the water and quinoa to a boil in a medium saucepan. Cover, reduce to a simmer and cook for 10 minutes. Turn the heat off and leave the covered saucepan on the burner for another 6 minutes. Fluff with a fork and set aside.

Place 2 tsp (10 mL) of the sesame oil in a large frying pan over medium heat. When the oil is hot, add the broccoli and onion and cover the pan. Stir frequently and add 1 Tbsp (15 mL) of water if the saucepan appears dry. Cook until the onion is opaque and the broccoli tender, about 8 to 10 minutes. Transfer to a bowl and set aside.

Remove the chicken, reserving the marinade. Place the remaining sesame oil and the chicken in the large saucepan on medium-high heat and cook until the chicken is no longer pink, about 7 to 8 minutes. Reduce the heat to medium and add the marinade to the pan. Stir in the water, peanut butter and honey and cook for 1 minute. Toss in the broccoli-onion mixture and stir thoroughly.

Divide the quinoa among individual serving plates. Top with the chicken-broccoli mixture. Sprinkle with toasted cashews and serve.

Serves 4.

Chicken Fried Quinoa

Traditionally made with rice, this recipe gets a healthy boost from the quinoa but is still packed with flavor. The amount of chicken in this dish makes it an entire meal on its own. Replace the chicken with tofu to make it vegetarian.

1⅓ cups (330 mL) water

⅔ cup (160 mL) quinoa

1 tsp (5 mL) vegetable oil

2 large eggs, beaten

2 Tbsp (30 mL) sesame oil

2½ cups (625 mL) diced chicken, shrimp, pork or tofu

1 tsp (5 mL) minced fresh garlic

½ cup (125 mL) diced celery

1 cup (250 mL) diced red bell pepper (about 1 pepper)

¾ cup (185 mL) frozen green peas, thawed

½ cup (125 mL) sliced green onion

¼ cup (60 mL) soy sauce or gluten-free tamari

Bring the water and quinoa to a boil in a medium saucepan. Cover, reduce to a simmer and cook for 10 minutes. Turn the heat off and leave the covered saucepan on the burner for another 6 minutes. Fluff with a fork and set aside.

Heat the vegetable oil in a large wok or saucepan on medium-high heat. Fry the beaten eggs as you would a large pancake, flipping once to cook both sides. Remove the egg from the pan, slice thinly and set aside.

Heat 1 Tbsp (15 mL) of the sesame oil in the same pan on medium-high heat. Fry the diced chicken with the garlic until browned and cooked through. Remove from the pan and set aside.

Reduce the heat to medium and add the remaining 1 Tbsp (15 mL) sesame oil. Sauté the celery for about 4 minutes. Add the red pepper and peas, cooking for another 3 minutes, until the vegetables are tender. Add the quinoa, green onion and soy sauce to the vegetables. Fold in the fried egg and the chicken and cook for 1 to 2 minutes to warm up the mixture. Adjust the seasoning if desired and serve immediately.

Makes 25.

Baked Chicken Nuggets

Chicken nuggets are always a favorite with children, and you can relax knowing these ones are wholesome and homemade. Serve them for supper or as an appetizer with your favorite dips. This recipe can be made with either chicken or turkey, but you will find that chicken makes a better, moister nugget. Dipping the pieces in butter before coating them makes a tender, crispy coating, but if you prefer leaner chicken nuggets, bake them without the butter.

½ cup (125 mL) water
¼ cup (60 mL) white or golden
    quinoa
1 lb (500 g) extralean ground
    chicken or turkey
1 tsp (5 mL) salt
½ cup (125 mL) dry breadcrumbs
    (or gluten-free breadcrumbs)

⅓ cup (80 mL) freshly grated
    Parmesan cheese
½ tsp (2 mL) dried thyme
½ tsp (2 mL) dried basil
½ cup (125 mL) butter, melted
    (optional)

Bring the water and quinoa to a boil in a small saucepan. Reduce to a simmer, cover and cook for 10 minutes. Turn the heat off and leave the covered saucepan on the burner for an additional 5 minutes. Remove the lid, fluff with a fork and set aside to cool.

Combine the ground meat with the quinoa and salt in a medium bowl. In a separate, shallow bowl combine the breadcrumbs, cheese, thyme and basil.

Preheat the oven to 400°F (200°C). Lightly grease a large baking sheet or spray with cooking oil. (Or line the baking sheet with parchment paper.) Create even-sized nuggets by using a tablespoon and forming the meat mixture into flat ovals, ½ inch (1 cm) thick. Dip the nuggets in butter (if using) then coat in the breadcrumb mixture and place on the baking sheet. Bake for 10 minutes on the center oven rack. Remove from the oven, flip the nuggets over and bake for an additional 10 minutes. Serve hot with any of your favorite dips.

Turkey-Stuffed Mozzarella Peppers

Loaded with turkey, quinoa and cheese, these peppers are filling. This dish is a meal in itself or can be served with a light salad or soup. To make this vegetarian, leave out the turkey and use a soy alternative instead.

⅓ cup (80 mL) quinoa
⅔ cup (160 mL) water
4 green bell peppers
1 lb (500 g) ground turkey
1 cup (250 mL) diced onion
1½ tsp (7.5 mL) Italian seasoning
1 tsp (5 mL) minced fresh garlic

3 Tbsp (45 mL) tomato paste
¼ cup (60 mL) freshly grated
  Parmesan cheese
½ cup (125 mL) water
1 cup (250 mL) shredded part-skim
  mozzarella cheese

Bring the quinoa and water to a boil in a small saucepan. Cover, reduce to a simmer and cook for 10 minutes. Turn off the heat and leave the covered saucepan on the burner for another 6 minutes. Fluff with a fork and set aside to cool.

Preheat the oven to 350°F (180°C). Grease a 9- × 13-inch (3.5 L) casserole dish or spray with cooking oil.

Bring a large saucepan of water to a boil. Cut the peppers in half lengthwise, removing the stems, seeds and membranes. Place them in the boiling water for 2 minutes, until they are tender-crisp. Remove and drain on a kitchen towel.

Place a large frying pan on medium-high heat. Add the turkey, onion, Italian seasoning and garlic. Sauté until the turkey is cooked and the onion is tender, about 8 minutes. Stir in the quinoa, tomato paste, Parmesan cheese and water, blending well.

Spoon the filling into the pepper halves and place them in the prepared dish. Sprinkle mozzarella cheese evenly over the top of each pepper. Bake for 15 to 20 minutes, until the peppers are tender and the filling is hot. Serve immediately.

Serves 4–6.

Apple-Glazed Pork Chops *on* Quinoa

This is a simple, family-friendly recipe. The flavor is best if marinated overnight before barbecuing. Great served with fresh steamed green beans or Brussels sprouts.

1 cup (250 mL) apple juice
¼ cup (60 mL) vegetable oil
3 Tbsp (45 mL) soy sauce or
   gluten-free tamari
1 tsp (5 mL) minced fresh garlic
1½ tsp (7.5 mL) grated fresh
   ginger
¼ tsp (1 mL) salt

6 pork loin chops
   (1 inch/2.5 cm thick)
3 cups (750 mL) water
1 cup (250 mL) quinoa
¾ cup (185 mL) packed brown
   sugar
2 Tbsp (30 mL) cornstarch
1 tsp (5 mL) sesame seeds

Combine the apple juice, oil, soy sauce, garlic, ginger and salt in a large resealable freezer bag or bowl and mix thoroughly. Add the pork chops and seal the bag. Place in the fridge overnight or for at least 2 hours.

Combine 2 cups (500 mL) of the water and the quinoa in a medium saucepan and bring to a boil. Reduce to a simmer, cover and cook for 10 minutes. Turn the heat off and leave the covered saucepan on the burner for another 6 minutes. Remove from the heat and fluff with a fork.

Drain the pork marinade into a medium saucepan. Add the remaining 1 cup (250 mL) of water and the brown sugar and whisk in the cornstarch. Cook on medium-high, whisking frequently, until it has bubbled for at least 1 minute and the mixture is clear and thick enough to coat the back of a spoon. Remove from the heat.

Lightly spray the barbecue grill with cooking oil and preheat to medium. Place the pork chops on the grill and barbecue for 5 to 6 minutes on each side. Glaze the pork with the sauce in the last few minutes of cooking. Remove the pork from the barbecue and allow to rest for 5 minutes before serving.

Place a bed of quinoa on individual serving plates. Arrange the pork chops on top of the quinoa and pour the sauce overtop. Sprinkle with sesame seeds and serve immediately.

Peruvian Peppered Steak *on* Quinoa

This quick and healthy recipe is inspired by Lomo Saltado, *a Peruvian beef and vegetable stir-fry dish traditionally served with rice and french fries.*

1 cup (250 mL) quinoa
2 cups (500 mL) water
2 Tbsp (30 mL) vegetable or
   olive oil
1 lb (500 g) beef sirloin, cut into
   ¾-inch-thick (2 cm) strips
¼ tsp (1 mL) ground black pepper
1½ cups (375 mL) thickly sliced
   red onion
1½ cups (375 mL) thickly sliced
   green bell pepper

2 Tbsp (30 mL) minced jalapeño
   pepper
2½ cups (625 mL) beef broth
¼ cup (60 mL) dry red wine
2 Tbsp (30 mL) cornstarch
1 cup (250 mL) halved cherry
   tomatoes
¼ cup (60 mL) chopped fresh
   cilantro
Cilantro sprigs (optional)

Bring the quinoa and water to a boil in a medium saucepan. Cover, reduce to a simmer and cook for 10 minutes. Turn the heat off and leave the covered saucepan on the burner for another 6 minutes. Fluff with a fork and set aside.

Heat a large saucepan on medium-high heat. Add 1 Tbsp (15 mL) of the oil, and when it's hot, add the beef strips. Season with black pepper and fry the meat for 5 to 7 minutes, until it's no longer pink. Remove the beef from the pan and set aside.

Add the remaining 1 Tbsp (15 mL) of oil to the hot saucepan and sauté the onion, green pepper and jalapeño for 7 to 10 minutes. Add 2 cups (500 mL) of the beef broth and the wine to the saucepan. Bring to a boil, then reduce the heat to low. Place the remaining ½ cup (125 mL) of beef broth in a small bowl and whisk in the cornstarch. Stir the mixture into the saucepan and cook until the sauce becomes transparent and coats the back of a spoon. Add the beef, tomatoes and cilantro to the saucepan.

To serve, divide the hot quinoa among individual plates. Arrange the peppered beef on top of the quinoa and serve immediately. Garnish with an extra sprig of cilantro, if desired.

Chili

This chili is made with meat, but simply leave it out or add a ground soy substitute for a vegetarian version. Serve it with your choice of garnishes and toppings. Freeze in individual containers for quick meals.

1 Tbsp (15 mL) olive oil
1 lb (500 g) ground lean beef, buffalo or turkey
1 cup (250 mL) diced white onion
1 cup (250 mL) diced green bell pepper (about 1 pepper)
1 tsp (5 mL) minced fresh garlic
One 28 oz (796 mL) can diced tomatoes
One 19 oz (540 mL) can black beans, drained and rinsed
One 14 oz (398 mL) can kidney beans, drained and rinsed
½ cup (125 mL) quinoa

One 5½ oz (156 mL) can tomato paste
1 cup (250 mL) water
3 Tbsp (45 mL) chili powder
1 tsp (5 mL) unsweetened cocoa powder
½ tsp (2 mL) dried oregano
¼ tsp (1 mL) ground cumin
¼ tsp (1 mL) salt
¼ tsp (1 mL) ground black pepper
2 Tbsp (30 mL) white vinegar
Sour cream, guacamole, cheddar cheese, green onion, tortilla chips (optional)

Heat the oil in a large saucepan on medium heat and cook the ground meat until completely browned. Stir in the onion, green pepper and garlic. Cover and cook for about 5 minutes, or until the onion starts to soften.

Add the tomatoes, black beans and kidney beans, quinoa, tomato paste and water. Mix in the chili powder, cocoa powder, oregano, cumin, salt and black pepper. Bring the mixture to a boil, then reduce to a simmer and cook uncovered for about 20 minutes. Remove from the heat and stir in the vinegar.

Serve immediately, garnishing with sour cream, guacamole, cheddar cheese, green onion and tortilla chips (if using).

Serves 6.

Roasted Vegetable Tilapia *on* Quinoa

Sweet balsamic vinegar and fresh roasted vegetables beautifully complement this light, mild-flavored fish that is baked in the oven.

2 cups (500 mL) water
1 cup (250 mL) quinoa
2 Tbsp (30 mL) olive or
    vegetable oil
¼ cup (60 mL) diced red onion
1½ cups (375 mL) quartered white
    button mushrooms
1 cup (250 mL) diced zucchini

1 cup (250 mL) diced red bell
    pepper (about 1 pepper)
2 tsp (10 mL) minced fresh garlic
½ tsp (2 mL) salt
Pinch ground black pepper
2 Tbsp (30 mL) balsamic vinegar
6 frozen tilapia fillets

Bring the water and quinoa to a boil in a medium saucepan. Cover, reduce to a simmer and cook for 10 minutes. Turn the heat off and leave the covered saucepan on the burner for another 6 minutes. Fluff with a fork and set aside.

Preheat the oven to 450°F (230°C). Lightly grease a 9- × 13-inch (3.5 L) baking dish, spray with cooking oil or line with parchment paper.

Heat the oil in a medium saucepan on medium-high heat. Add the onion and sauté for about 3 minutes. Add the mushrooms, zucchini, red pepper, garlic, salt and pepper. Sauté for another 3 minutes. Remove from the heat and toss with the balsamic vinegar. Set aside.

Place the frozen tilapia fillets in the baking dish and spoon the vegetable mixture over the fillets. Bake uncovered for about 20 minutes on the center rack (the fish will be done when it's opaque and flakes easily). Remove from the oven. To serve, divide the quinoa among individual serving plates and top with the fish. Serve immediately.

Serves 4.

Salmon *and* Red Quinoa *on* Asparagus *with* Lime Cilantro Sauce

The tender green of asparagus, red quinoa and pink salmon make this heart-healthy dish bold both in flavor and color.

⅓ cup (80 mL) red quinoa
⅔ cup (160 mL) water
½ cup (125 mL) light sour cream
3 Tbsp (45 mL) light mayonnaise
1 tsp (5 mL) grated lime zest
2 Tbsp (30 mL) fresh lime juice
1 tsp (5 mL) grated fresh ginger
1 Tbsp (15 mL) minced fresh
   cilantro

Pinch salt
Four 4 oz (100 g) fresh wild salmon
   fillets (about 1 inch/2.5 cm
   thick)
1 lb (500 g) asparagus
1 Tbsp (15 mL) butter

Bring the quinoa and water to a boil in a small saucepan. Reduce to a simmer, cover and cook for 10 minutes. Turn the heat off but keep the covered saucepan on the burner for an additional 6 minutes. Remove the lid and fluff with a fork. Set aside.

Combine the sour cream, mayonnaise, lime zest, 1 Tbsp (15 mL) of the lime juice, ginger, cilantro and salt in a small bowl, mixing well. Set aside.

Preheat the oven to 375°F (190°C). Place the fillets on a foil-lined baking sheet and brush with oil. Place in the oven and bake uncovered on the center rack for about 11 to 14 minutes (the salmon will be pink and flake easily with a fork).

While the salmon is cooking, prepare the asparagus. Trim off the tough portion of each spear by grasping it and bending it near the bottom third. The asparagus will snap where it begins to get tough. Place the asparagus in a large pot of boiling water and cook for about 3 to 5 minutes, until tender but crisp. Toss the asparagus in the butter and the remaining 1 Tbsp (15 mL) of lime juice. Season with additional salt to taste.

Arrange the asparagus on individual serving plates. Place a portion of the quinoa over the asparagus and top with a piece of salmon. Drizzle the lime dressing over the salmon and serve immediately.

Tasty Tuna Casserole

This version of a family recipe popular in many North American households is made from scratch.

2 cups (500 mL) water

1 cup (250 mL) quinoa

3 Tbsp (45 mL) butter

¾ cup (185 mL) finely diced white onion

¾ cup (185 mL) finely diced celery

2 cups (500 mL) chopped white button mushrooms

½ tsp (2 mL) minced fresh garlic

2 cups (500 mL) milk

¼ cup (60 mL) quinoa flour

¼ tsp (1 mL) salt

Pinch ground black pepper

Two 6 oz (170 g) cans flaked light tuna, drained

1 cup (250 mL) frozen peas, thawed

1¼ cups (310 mL) shredded cheddar cheese

¼ cup (60 mL) thinly sliced green onion

Bring the water and quinoa to a boil in a medium saucepan. Cover, reduce to a simmer and cook for 10 minutes. Turn the heat off and leave the covered saucepan on the burner for another 6 minutes. Fluff with a fork and allow the quinoa to cool.

Preheat the oven to 350°F (180°C). Lightly spray with cooking oil or grease a 9- × 13-inch (3.5 L) casserole dish.

Melt 1 Tbsp (15 mL) of the butter in a large saucepan. Sauté the white onion and celery until the onion becomes translucent, about 8 minutes. Add the mushrooms and garlic and continue to sauté until the vegetables are tender, another 5 minutes. Remove from the heat and set aside.

Combine the remaining 2 Tbsp (30 mL) butter, milk, flour, salt and pepper in a medium saucepan. Cook on medium-high heat, stirring frequently, until thickened, about 5 minutes. Remove the saucepan from the heat.

Add the quinoa to the vegetable mixture in the large saucepan, along with the sauce, tuna, peas and 1 cup (250 mL) of the cheese. Stir to combine well and pour the mixture into the casserole dish. Top with the remaining ¼ cup (60 mL) of cheese and the green onion. Place on the center rack of the oven and bake for 25 minutes, until bubbling hot.

Serves 2.

Pepper Shrimp Quinoa

This flavorful, protein-packed shrimp dish is fabulously light but holds its own as an entire meal. It also makes a great side for almost anything. For a vegetarian version, use 2 cups (500 mL) rinsed, drained canned soybeans instead of shrimp. This recipe is best with the generous use of fresh herbs, but if you don't have them, use 2 tsp (10 mL) each of dried basil and thyme instead and add them with the cream. If you want more vegetables, add as many as you like to this dish.

½ cup (125 mL) quinoa
1 cup (250 mL) water
1 cup (250 mL) half and half cream (10–12%)
½ tsp (2 mL) Worcestershire sauce
½ cup (125 mL) white wine
2 Tbsp (30 mL) chopped fresh sweet basil
2 Tbsp (30 mL) chopped fresh thyme
⅔ cup (160 mL) freshly grated Parmesan cheese

1 Tbsp (15 mL) vegetable oil
1 cup (250 mL) finely chopped white onion
1 tsp (5 mL) minced fresh garlic
1 large red bell pepper, diced
1 lb (500 g) peeled cooked shrimp (fresh, or thawed if frozen)
½ cup (125 mL) raw, unsalted pumpkin seeds

Bring the quinoa and water to a boil in a medium saucepan. Reduce to a simmer, cover and cook for 10 minutes. Turn the heat off and leave the covered saucepan on the burner for an additional 4 minutes. Remove the lid and fluff with a fork. Set aside.

Whisk the cream, Worcestershire sauce and wine in a medium saucepan and cook over medium-low heat for 4 minutes. Stir in the basil, thyme and cheese. Simmer on low for an additional 3 minutes.

Heat the oil in a large skillet over medium heat. Add the onion and sauté for 5 minutes. Stir in the garlic and red pepper and cook for another 3 to 4 minutes, until the onion is opaque and tender. Add the shrimp, cooked quinoa and pumpkin seeds. Sauté until heated throughout. Top with the Parmesan sauce and serve immediately.

You can make this the night before you serve it. Store the sauce and the quinoa-shrimp mixture in separate sealed containers in the refrigerator. When ready to serve, simply reheat.

Makes 20.

Easy Quinoa Temaki

Temaki, or "handroll," is handheld sushi in the shape of a cone. It is the easiest sushi to make and dramatically decorates any party platter. Since it is best made immediately before serving, make the rolls just before a party, or let guests roll their own and choose their own fillings. Serve with wasabi, ginger and tamari or soy sauce on the side. This is our favorite combination of flavors, but feel free to try your own ideas. Instead of crab or tofu, try tuna or salmon (as pictured), or shrimp. Enoki mushrooms are also a nice addition. To make this recipe gluten-free, use tamari instead of soy sauce and real crabmeat instead of imitation.

2 cups (500 mL) water
1 cup (250 mL) white or golden
   quinoa
6 Tbsp (90 mL) white rice vinegar
1½ tsp (7.5 mL) liquid honey
¼ tsp (1 mL) salt
One 10-sheet package (1 oz/28 g)
   dried sushi nori
1 avocado, sliced into 20 strips
¼ cup (60 mL) julienne or
   shredded carrot

1 Tbsp (15 mL) sliced pickled
   ginger, cut into thin strips
1 cup (250 mL) real or imitation
   crabmeat (or 2 eggs, whisked,
   fried and cut into strips, or
   strips of extrafirm tofu)
2 Tbsp (30 mL) black or white
   toasted sesame seeds
Tamari (gluten-free) or soy sauce
Wasabi (if using)

Bring the water and quinoa to a boil in a medium saucepan. Reduce to a simmer, cover and cook for 10 minutes. Turn the heat off and leave the covered saucepan on the burner for an additional 10 minutes to allow residual heat in the pot to continue cooking the quinoa to an extra-plump texture. Fluff with a fork and set aside.

Meanwhile, heat the vinegar, honey and salt in a small saucepan or in the microwave until the mixture is warm and the honey and salt are dissolved. Stir the vinegar mixture into the warm quinoa until evenly distributed. Allow the quinoa to cool to room temperature in the un-covered pot.

Continued on page 102 . . .

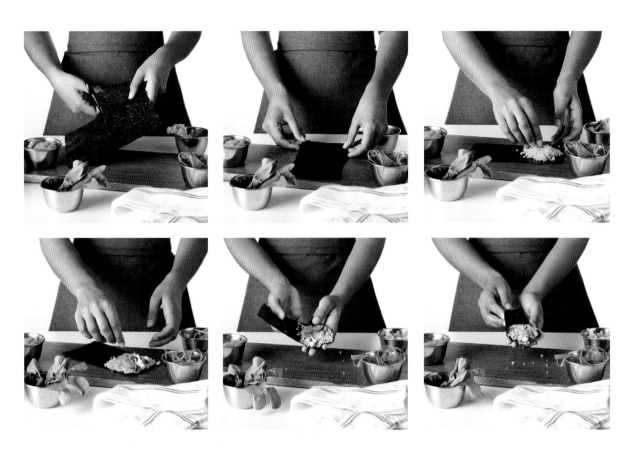

Ensuring your hands are dry, cut a piece of nori in half with scissors. Place 1 piece of nori on a cutting surface or counter with the rough side facing up.

Place 2 Tbsp (30 mL) of the quinoa on the left half of the nori and spread slightly, leaving a ½-inch (1 cm) border around the sides. Add a strip each of avocado, carrot and pickled ginger. Set a piece of crabmeat (or egg or tofu) on top.

Take the bottom left corner of the nori and bring it up to the center top. Keep rolling it around until the nori forms a cone. Using your finger dipped in water, moisten the inner edge of the nori and press gently together to seal. Sprinkle the top of each temaki with a few sesame seeds. As you are putting the temaki on a plate or platter, place a weight (such as the edge of a saucer) on the side of the nori to hold down the edges until set. Repeat with the remaining ingredients.

Serve the temaki immediately. Serve tamari or soy sauce and wasabi on the side.

Broccoli Goat Cheese Soufflé

Although Dijon, rosemary and goat cheese make this recipe sound fancy, it is simple and tasty, and looks great alongside a salad. The recipe calls for red quinoa, but you can use any color and it will still be an exciting dish.

½ cup (125 mL) water	1 tsp (5 mL) Dijon mustard
¼ cup (60 mL) red quinoa	¼ tsp (1 mL) dried rosemary
2 cups (500 mL) finely chopped broccoli florets	½ cup (125 mL) crumbled goat cheese
1 Tbsp (15 mL) butter	3 large eggs, separated
1 Tbsp (15 mL) extra virgin olive oil	2 large egg whites
2 Tbsp (30 mL) quinoa flour	¼ tsp (1 mL) cream of tartar
1¼ cups (310 mL) low-fat milk	3 sprigs fresh rosemary (optional)

Bring the water and quinoa to a boil in a small saucepan. Reduce to a simmer, cover and cook for 10 minutes. Turn the heat off and leave the covered saucepan on the burner for an additional 5 minutes. Remove the lid and fluff with a fork. Set aside to cool.

Preheat the oven to 375°F (190°C). Grease an 8-inch (20 cm) round soufflé or casserole dish or spray with cooking oil.

Steam the broccoli on the stove or in a microwave oven until slightly tender. Set aside.

Melt the butter and oil in a large saucepan over medium-high heat. Whisk in the flour and continue to whisk and cook for 2 minutes. Add the milk, mustard and rosemary and whisk constantly until thickened, 1 to 2 minutes. Remove from the heat and immediately whisk in the goat cheese, ½ cup (125 mL) cooked quinoa and 3 egg yolks until well combined. Transfer the mixture to a large bowl.

In a separate, medium bowl, beat the 5 egg whites with an electric mixer on high speed until soft peaks form. Add the cream of tartar and continue beating until stiff peaks form. Using a rubber spatula, gently fold half of the whipped whites into the milk mixture. Gently fold in the remaining egg whites and the reserved broccoli until no white streaks remain. Transfer to the casserole dish.

Bake for 30 minutes on the center oven rack, until the soufflé is puffed and firm to the touch. Garnish with rosemary if using. Serve immediately.

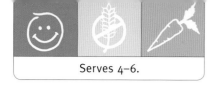

Soufflé Monterey

A great anytime dish that is quick to prepare, as long as you think ahead and drain the zucchini the night before. Colored quinoa, especially black, gives this light and fluffy soufflé a unique appearance.

4 cups (1 L) peeled and shredded
   zucchini
1 cup (250 mL) water
½ cup (125 mL) quinoa
4 large eggs
¼ tsp (1 mL) ground black pepper
¼ tsp (1 mL) garlic powder

½ tsp (2 mL) salt
2 Tbsp (30 mL) chopped fresh
   parsley
½ cup (125 mL) diced red bell
   pepper
1 cup (250 mL) shredded Monterey
   Jack cheese

Place the peeled and shredded zucchini in a large strainer with a bowl underneath; drain overnight to remove the excess liquid.

Bring the water and quinoa to a boil in a small saucepan. Reduce to a simmer, cover and cook for 10 minutes. Turn the heat off and leave the covered saucepan on the burner for an additional 5 minutes. Remove the lid and fluff with a fork. Set aside to cool.

Preheat the oven to 350°F (180°C). Spray or lightly grease a 9-inch (23 cm) round casserole dish.

Whisk the eggs, pepper, garlic powder, salt and parsley in a large bowl. Add the drained zucchini, quinoa, red pepper and cheese; mix until well blended.

Pour into the casserole dish and bake on the center oven rack for 50 to 60 minutes, until the top is nicely browned and the center is firm to the touch. Place on the stovetop to cool and set for at least 10 minutes prior to serving.

Serves 4–6.

Tomato *and* Basil Crustless Quiche

A savory and warm home-style dish that is quick to throw together. If you prefer a crust, use this recipe to fill any of your usual pastry recipes.

⅔ cup (160 mL) water
⅓ cup (80 mL) quinoa
1 tsp (5 mL) vegetable or olive oil
1 cup (250 mL) diced onion
¼ cup (60 mL) quinoa flour or all-purpose flour
4 large eggs
2 Tbsp (30 mL) minced fresh basil (or 2 tsp/10 mL dried)
1½ cups (375 mL) seeded and diced Roma tomatoes (about 3)

¼ cup (60 mL) milk or half and half cream (10–12%)
1 cup (250 mL) shredded mozzarella cheese
⅓ cup (80 mL) freshly grated Parmesan cheese
¼ tsp (1 mL) salt
Pinch ground black pepper

Bring the water and quinoa to a boil in a small saucepan. Reduce to a simmer, cover and cook for 10 minutes. Turn the heat off and leave the covered saucepan on the burner for an additional 5 minutes. Remove the lid and fluff with a fork. Set aside.

Preheat the oven to 350°F (180°C). Lightly grease a 9-inch (23 cm) round baking dish or spray with cooking oil.

Heat the oil in a large skillet on medium-low heat. Sauté the onion until tender and opaque, about 10 minutes.

Whisk together the flour and eggs. Add the quinoa, basil, tomatoes, milk, mozzarella and Parmesan cheese, salt, pepper and sautéed onion; mix well. Pour into the prepared dish and bake for 50 minutes on the center oven rack, until the center is firm. Remove from the oven and cool for 10 minutes. Run a knife around the outside edge of the quiche. Slice into wedges and serve hot or cold. Refrigerate leftovers for a quick next-day lunch or dinner.

Vegetable Cheddar Quiche

An uncomplicated, effortless dish. Mix it up and create your own version by substituting your favorite vegetables for the broccoli.

Crust	1 cup (250 mL) quinoa flour	1 Tbsp (15 mL) water
	½ cup (125 mL) butter, melted and slightly cooled	

Filling	1 Tbsp (15 mL) butter	4 large eggs
	2 cups (500 mL) chopped fresh broccoli or asparagus	¼ cup (60 mL) milk
	1 cup (250 mL) finely chopped onion	1 Tbsp (15 mL) quinoa flour
	1 tsp (5 mL) minced fresh garlic	½ tsp (2 mL) salt
	1 cup (250 mL) shredded aged cheddar cheese	¼ tsp (1 mL) ground black pepper

Preheat the oven to 350°F (180°C). Place the quinoa flour and butter in a medium bowl and mix well. Add the water, and make a soft dough using your hands. Grease a 9-inch (23 cm) round baking dish or spray with cooking oil. Press the mixture evenly into the dish. Set aside.

For the filling, melt the butter in a medium saucepan over medium-low heat and sauté the broccoli, onion and garlic for about 8 minutes, until the vegetables are tender. Spoon the vegetables evenly over the crust and sprinkle with the cheese.

Whisk the eggs, milk, quinoa flour, salt and pepper in a medium bowl. Pour the mixture over the vegetables.

Bake the quiche on the center oven rack for 30 minutes, or until the center is set. Let stand 8 to 10 minutes before cutting into wedges. Serve immediately. Refrigerate leftovers for up to 3 days.

Cheese *and* Spinach Frittata

Very easy to make, this dish is brimming with calcium and protein. It can be made with any cheese but tastes best with a sharp, aged cheddar cheese.

¼ cup (60 mL) quinoa
½ cup (125 mL) water
4 large eggs
¾ cup (185 mL) finely diced ham
1 cup (250 mL) cottage
    cheese (2%)

One 10 oz (300 g) package
    chopped frozen spinach,
    thawed and drained
1½ cups (375 mL) shredded aged
    cheddar cheese

Bring the quinoa and water to a boil in a medium saucepan. Cover, reduce to a simmer and cook for 10 minutes. Turn off the heat and leave the covered saucepan on the burner for another 6 minutes. Fluff with a fork and allow the quinoa to cool.

Preheat the oven to 350°F (180°C). Grease a 9-inch (23 cm) round casserole dish or spray with cooking oil.

Beat the eggs in a large bowl. Stir in the quinoa, ham, cottage cheese, spinach and cheddar cheese and pour the mixture into the casserole dish. Bake on the center oven rack for 50 to 60 minutes, or until the center is firm and the edges are golden brown. Remove from the oven and let sit for 10 minutes to cool slightly before cutting into wedges. Serve hot or cold.

Serves 4.

Spanikopita Frittata

This crustless dish inspired by the savory Greek pastry of the same name is filled with chopped spinach, onion, feta and eggs.

1 Tbsp (15 mL) olive oil

1 cup (250 mL) finely chopped green or white onion

One 10 oz (300 g) package chopped frozen spinach, thawed and drained

4 large eggs

½ cup (125 mL) quinoa flour

1½ cups (375 mL) cottage cheese (2%)

1½ cups (375 mL) crumbled feta cheese

2 Tbsp (30 mL) chopped fresh dill

1 tsp (5 mL) minced fresh garlic

¼ tsp (1 mL) salt

¼ tsp (1 mL) ground black pepper

Preheat the oven to 350°F (180°C). Spray a 9-inch (23 cm) round baking dish with cooking oil or grease the dish.

Heat the oil in a large saucepan on medium-low heat and sauté the onion until tender. Stir in the spinach and continue to cook until there is no excess water, about 4 to 5 minutes. Remove from the heat and cool for about 5 minutes.

Whisk the eggs and quinoa flour in a medium bowl until smoothly blended. Add the spinach, cottage cheese, feta cheese, dill, garlic, salt and pepper and mix thoroughly. Combine the spinach mixture with the egg mixture and pour into the casserole dish. Bake on the center oven rack for about 50 to 60 minutes, until the center is firm. Remove from the oven and let rest for 10 minutes to set. Divide into 8 pieces and serve.

Quinoa Veggie Bake

A flavorful dish, full of healthy vegetables. Serve it as a complete meal or with your choice of salad.

1 cup (250 mL) quinoa
2 cups (500 mL) water
2 Tbsp (30 mL) butter
1 cup (250 mL) diced onion
3 cups (750 mL) broccoli florets
¼ tsp (1 mL) salt
2 cups (500 mL) sliced white
   button mushrooms
1 cup (250 mL) chopped red bell
   pepper (about 1 pepper)

1 tsp (5 mL) basil pesto
2 large eggs
1 cup (250 mL) shredded cheddar
   cheese
1 cup (250 mL) ricotta cheese
½ cup (125 mL) light sour cream
¼ tsp (1 mL) ground black pepper
¼ cup (60 mL) cheddar cheese
   (optional)

Preheat the oven to 350°F (180°C). Spray with cooking oil or grease a 9- × 13-inch (3.5 L) casserole dish.

Bring the quinoa and water to a boil in a small saucepan. Reduce to a simmer, cover and cook for 10 minutes. Turn the heat off and leave the covered saucepan on the burner for an additional 6 minutes. Remove the lid and fluff with a fork. Set aside.

Melt the butter in a large pot over medium heat. Add the onion and cook until softened and opaque, about 5 minutes. Stir in the broccoli, salt and 1 to 2 Tbsp (15 to 30 mL) of water to facilitate cooking if necessary. Sauté for 2 minutes, then add the mushrooms, red pepper and pesto. Cook until the mushrooms are just softened, 4 to 5 minutes. Remove from the heat and stir in the quinoa.

Beat the eggs in a medium bowl and stir in the cheddar cheese, ricotta and sour cream. Mix well. Season with pepper and fold into the vegetable-quinoa mixture. Spread into the prepared casserole dish and top with shredded cheese if desired. Bake on the center oven rack for 30 to 35 minutes or until the center is hot. Refrigerate leftovers for up to 3 days.

Southwestern Quinoa

Topped with melted cheddar cheese and a dollop of tangy lime yogurt, this scrumptious and simple meal can also be served as a side dish.

2 cups (500 mL) water
1 cup (250 mL) quinoa
¾ cup (185 mL) prepared salsa,
　hot or medium
¼ tsp (1 mL) chili powder
¼ tsp (1 mL) ground coriander
¼ tsp (1 mL) ground cumin
1 Tbsp (15 mL) finely chopped
　fresh cilantro

1 cup (250 mL) diced tomato
1 cup (250 mL) cooked black beans
½ cup (125 mL) corn kernels
½ cup (125 mL) plain yogurt
1 tsp (5 mL) fresh lime juice
1 cup (250 mL) shredded aged
　cheddar cheese
1 avocado, sliced

Bring the water and quinoa to a boil in a medium saucepan. Cover, reduce to a simmer and cook for 10 minutes. Turn the heat off and leave the covered saucepan on the burner for another 6 minutes. Fluff with a fork.

Add the salsa, chili powder, coriander and cumin to the quinoa and mix well. Mix in the cilantro, tomato, beans and corn, stirring until all the ingredients are evenly blended.

In a small bowl, whisk together the yogurt and lime juice. Spoon the quinoa mixture into individual serving dishes and top with shredded cheese and a generous spoonful of the lime yogurt. Garnish with avocado slices.

Mexican Casserole

Enjoy the flavors of Mexico with this versatile dish. If you prefer, use potatoes instead of zucchini, or for a nonvegetarian version, substitute cooked ground beef, chicken or turkey.

Taco seasoning

1 Tbsp (15 mL) chili powder
1½ tsp (7.5 mL) ground cumin
½ tsp (2 mL) salt
¼ tsp (1 mL) ground black pepper
¼ tsp (1 mL) dried oregano
¼ tsp (1 mL) garlic powder
Pinch cayenne pepper

Casserole

1 cup (250 mL) water
½ cup (125 mL) quinoa
2 cups (500 mL) diced zucchini
1 medium red bell pepper, diced
1 medium green bell pepper, diced
One 14 oz (398 mL) can black beans or navy beans
¼ cup (60 mL) sliced green onion
1 cup (250 mL) prepared salsa (mild, medium or hot)
1 cup (250 mL) shredded aged cheddar cheese
⅓ cup (80 mL) sliced black olives
Light sour cream (optional)

Combine all the ingredients for the taco seasoning in a small bowl. Set aside.

Bring the water and quinoa to a boil in a small saucepan. Reduce to a simmer, cover and cook for 10 minutes. Turn the heat off and leave the covered saucepan on the burner for an additional 4 minutes. Remove the lid and fluff with a fork. Set aside.

Preheat the oven to 350°F (180°C). Grease a 9- × 13-inch (3.5 L) casserole dish and spread the zucchini and red and green peppers in the bottom. Sprinkle with 1 tsp (5 mL) of the taco seasoning.

Combine the beans, cooked quinoa, green onion and 1 Tbsp (15 mL) of taco seasoning and mix well. A small amount of taco seasoning will be left over, but it is not required for the recipe. Place the bean-quinoa mixture over the vegetables in the baking dish. Spread a layer of salsa on top of the quinoa mixture, then top with the cheese and black olives. Bake on the center oven rack for 25 to 30 minutes, until the cheese has melted and the casserole is hot throughout. Serve immediately and top with sour cream (if using).

Cheesy Spinach *and* Quinoa Stuffed Pasta

Occasionally we all like to treat ourselves to comfort food. This is a feel-good kind of meal with boosted nutrition from the quinoa and spinach.

⅓ cup (80 mL) quinoa
⅔ cup (160 mL) water
One 12 oz (355 g) box jumbo
 pasta shells
2 large eggs
1½ cups (375 mL) shredded part-
 skim mozzarella cheese
1 cup (250 mL) ricotta cheese
¾ cup (185 mL) freshly grated
 Parmesan cheese

One 10 oz (300 g) package chopped
 frozen spinach, thawed and
 squeezed almost dry
¼ tsp (1 mL) salt
Pinch ground black pepper
3 cups (750 mL) tomato sauce
 (your choice)

Bring the quinoa and water to a boil in a medium saucepan. Cover, reduce to a simmer and cook for 10 minutes. Turn the heat off and leave the covered saucepan on the burner for another 6 minutes. Fluff with a fork and allow the quinoa to cool.

Preheat the oven to 350°F (180°C). Cook the pasta shells according to the directions on the box.

Beat the eggs. Add the quinoa with the mozzarella, ricotta, Parmesan, spinach, salt and pepper.

Spread the tomato sauce with the back of a spoon over the bottom of a 9- × 13-inch (3.5 L) casserole dish. Fill each pasta shell with about 2 to 3 Tbsp (30 to 45 mL) of the cheese mixture and place in the casserole dish, beginning at one corner of the dish. (A few shells may be left over.) Cover with foil and bake on the center oven rack for 20 minutes. Remove the foil and bake for an additional 10 minutes, until the pasta is slightly golden and the sauce is bubbling.

Serves 4.

Serves 1.

Chicken Sprout Salad Wrap

The crunch of quinoa sprouts gives a different take on the usual chicken salad wrap. Use brown rice tortillas for a gluten-free version.

2 cups (500 mL) diced, cooked chicken or turkey
½ cup (125 mL) dried cranberries
½ cup (125 mL) toasted slivered almonds
¼ cup (60 mL) finely diced celery
½ cup (125 mL) quinoa sprouts (page 56)
3 Tbsp (45 mL) thinly sliced green onion
½ cup (125 mL) plain yogurt
½ cup (125 mL) low-fat mayonnaise
¼ tsp (1 mL) salt
Pinch ground black pepper
4 large soft whole wheat tortillas (10 inches/
    25 cm) or 8 small (8 inches/20 cm)
¼ cup (60 mL) shredded cheddar cheese
    (optional)

Combine the chicken, cranberries, almonds, celery, sprouts and green onion in a large bowl. Add the yogurt, mayonnaise, salt and pepper. Stir until thoroughly mixed. Place about 1 cup (250 mL) of the filling on each large wrap or ½ cup (125 mL) on the small wraps. Sprinkle the cheddar cheese on top, if using. Fold and serve.

Supreme Turkey Sprout Sandwich

Treat yourself to a hearty homemade deli sandwich, fully loaded with roasted red pepper, quinoa sprouts, onion, turkey and havarti. To make this gluten-free, use gluten-free bread. Prefer the vegetarian option? Leave out the turkey and this sandwich is still fabulous.

2 slices whole wheat (or gluten-free) bread
2 tsp (10 mL) light mayonnaise
2 Tbsp (30 mL) quinoa sprouts (page 56)
2 slices turkey
1 slice havarti cheese
1 slice roasted red pepper
2 slices red onion
1 tsp (5 mL) Dijon mustard

Spread 1 piece of the bread with mayonnaise and sprinkle the quinoa sprouts evenly on top. Add the turkey slices, havarti, roasted red pepper and red onion. Spread the Dijon on the other piece of bread and place on top of the sandwich.

Cucumber Gouda Sprout Sandwich

Add your favorite soup to create a meal with this crisp, refreshing sandwich.

2 Tbsp (30 mL) light cream cheese, softened
1 tsp (5 mL) chopped fresh dill (or ¼ tsp/1 mL dried)
2 slices rye, whole wheat or gluten-free bread

4 slices cucumber
2 Tbsp (30 mL) quinoa sprouts (page 56)
½ tsp (2 mL) balsamic vinegar
2 rings sliced red onion
1 slice Gouda cheese

Combine the cream cheese and dill and spread on each slice of bread. Place the cucumber on 1 side. Toss the quinoa sprouts in the balsamic vinegar and place on top of the cucumber. Add the red onion and top with the Gouda cheese and the remaining slice of bread.

Serves 1.

Serves 2.

Egg Salad Sandwich

A good, solid high-protein sandwich that makes a fine light meal. Aside from the vibrant colors, the wow factor in this sandwich is the living quinoa sprouts.

1 large hard-boiled egg (shelled)
1 Tbsp (15 mL) light mayonnaise
2 tsp (10 mL) thinly sliced green onion
2 tsp (10 mL) minced fresh or roasted red pepper
Salt and ground black pepper to taste
2 slices pumpernickel, whole wheat or
    gluten-free bread
2–3 Tbsp (30–45 mL) quinoa sprouts (page 56)

Mash the egg in a shallow bowl with a fork. Mix in the mayonnaise, onion and red pepper. Season with salt and pepper. Spread the filling over 1 slice of bread. Sprinkle with the quinoa sprouts and top with the second slice of bread. Slice the sandwich diagonally and serve.

Tuna Basil Sprout Sandwich

The basil pesto, roasted red pepper and quinoa sprouts raise this tuna salad up several notches.

One 6 oz (170 g) can flaked or chunk light
    tuna in water, drained
3 Tbsp (45 mL) light mayonnaise
1½ tsp (7.5 mL) basil pesto
1 Tbsp (15 mL) thinly sliced green onion
4 slices bread (your choice)
¼ cup (60 mL) quinoa sprouts (page 56)
2 slices roasted red pepper (optional)

Place the tuna, mayonnaise, pesto and green onion in a small bowl and mix thoroughly. Spread half the mixture evenly on a slice of bread. Top with half the quinoa sprouts. Add 1 slice of roasted red pepper (if using) and top with another slice of bread. Repeat with the remaining ingredients to make a second sandwich. Serve immediately.

Serves 4–6.

Greek Burgers

Nothing against the regular burger, but this Greek version is outrageously good. These are best cooked on an outdoor grill, but if the weather doesn't cooperate, cook them on your indoor grill or in a frying pan. To make this gluten-free, ensure you use gluten-free buns or bread.

Patties		
¼ cup (60 mL) white or golden quinoa	¼ cup (60 mL) finely chopped green bell pepper	
½ cup (125 mL) water	¼ cup (60 mL) Greek- or Mediterranean-style salad dressing	
1 lb (500 g) lean ground beef		
½ cup (125 mL) chopped black olives	1 large egg	

Burgers		
4–6 buns, halved and lightly buttered	4–6 slices tomato	
¾ cup (185 mL) crumbled light feta cheese	4–6 slices red onion	
¼ cup (60 mL) light mayonnaise or tzatziki sauce	8–12 slices cucumber	

Bring the quinoa and water to a boil in a small saucepan. Reduce to a simmer, cover and cook for 10 minutes. Turn the heat off and leave the covered saucepan on the burner for an additional 6 minutes. Remove the lid and fluff with a fork. Set aside to cool.

Combine the ground meat, olives, green pepper, dressing, egg and ½ cup (125 mL) of the cooked quinoa. Form the mixture into 6 regular or 4 large hamburger patties, 1 inch (2.5 cm) thick, and place on a preheated barbecue. Cook 4 minutes on each side or until no longer pink. Place the halved buns face down on the grill and toast for 30 to 45 seconds, until slightly browned. Remove the buns and place a burger patty in each one. Sprinkle the crumbled feta evenly over the patties. Garnish with mayonnaise or tzatziki, tomato, onion and cucumber. Serve immediately.

Light Open-Faced Salmon Burgers

A light, inexpensive meal that will satisfy a big appetite. Use a gluten-free bread instead of English muffins to make this recipe gluten-free.

Patties	⅔ cup (160 mL) water	2 large eggs
	⅓ cup (80 mL) quinoa	1 Tbsp (15 mL) fresh dill (or 1 tsp/
	One 7½ oz (213 mL) can wild	5 mL dried dill)
	Pacific salmon (drained, larger	½ tsp (2 mL) minced fresh garlic
	bones removed)	Pinch ground black pepper
	½ cup (125 mL) sliced green onion	

Burgers	⅓ cup (80 mL) light cream cheese,	½ cup (125 mL) fresh spinach
	softened	leaves
	1 tsp (5 mL) grated lime zest	6 slices tomato
	1 tsp (5 mL) fresh lime juice	6 large slices Gouda cheese
	3 whole wheat English muffins (or	
	gluten-free bread)	

Bring the water and quinoa to a boil in a small saucepan. Cover, reduce to a simmer and cook for 10 minutes. Turn the heat off and leave the covered saucepan on the burner for another 6 minutes. Fluff with a fork and allow to cool.

Preheat the oven to 400°F (200°C). Combine the salmon, quinoa, green onion, eggs, dill, garlic and pepper in a medium bowl and mix well. Divide into 6 even portions and form into patties.

Grease a baking sheet or spray with cooking oil (or line with parchment paper). Arrange the salmon patties so they are evenly spaced on the baking sheet. Bake for 7 minutes and remove from the oven. Flip the patties over and bake for another 7 minutes.

Combine the cream cheese with the lime zest and juice in a small bowl. Mix well and set aside.

Toast the English muffins and spread with the cream cheese mixture. Place a few spinach leaves and a tomato slice on each. Top each with a hot salmon patty and a slice of cheese. Serve immediately.

Serves 6–8.

The Garden Burger

This is the ultimate meatless burger. Top with your favorite condiments, including cheese, mustard, mayonnaise, dark leafy lettuce or spinach and a hearty slice of tomato.

¼ cup (60 mL) quinoa

¼ cup (60 mL) dried green lentils

1½ cups (375 mL) water

⅓ cup (80 mL) finely chopped walnuts

½ cup (125 mL) fresh breadcrumbs (gluten-free if desired)

One 19 oz (540 mL) can chickpeas, drained and rinsed

¾ cup (185 mL) finely chopped celery

¾ cup (185 mL) finely chopped onion

1 cup (250 mL) finely chopped green or red bell pepper (about 1 pepper)

¼ tsp (1 mL) ground black pepper

Combine the quinoa, lentils and water in a small saucepan and bring to a boil. Cover, reduce to a simmer and cook for 23 minutes, or until the lentils are tender. Remove from the heat and set aside to cool.

Preheat the oven to 350°F (180°C) and lightly grease a baking sheet, spray with cooking oil or line with parchment paper. Combine the walnuts, breadcrumbs, chickpeas, celery, onion, green pepper and black pepper. Add the cooked lentils and quinoa.

Using your hands, thoroughly mix the ingredients together, breaking up the chickpeas. Using about ½ cup (125 mL) of the mixture at a time, shape into burger patties, placing them on the baking sheet. Bake on the center oven rack for 20 minutes. Serve with burger buns (gluten-free if desired) and the condiments of your choice.

Makes three 12-inch (30 cm) pizza crusts.

Outrageously Quick *and* Easy Pizza Crust

This pizza crust is fail-proof, light, tender and enhanced with whole quinoa grains. The white quinoa is virtually invisible and does not change the flavor of this classic pizza crust. Impress your family with this fantastic crust, but don't reveal the quinoa secret until after you've enjoyed it. This dough can be divided and frozen for an easy midweek meal.

1⅓ cups (330 mL) water
⅔ cup (160 mL) white quinoa
1½ cups (375 mL) warm water
2 Tbsp (30 mL) white or cane sugar
3 Tbsp (45 mL) vegetable or
 olive oil

½ tsp (2 mL) salt
1 Tbsp (15 mL) quick-rise yeast
 (1 envelope)
1 large egg, beaten
3½–4 cups (875 mL–1 L)
 all-purpose flour

Combine the 1⅓ cups (330 mL) water and quinoa in a medium saucepan and bring to a boil. Cover, reduce to a simmer and cook for 10 minutes. Turn the heat off and leave the covered saucepan on the burner for another 20 minutes. Fluff with a fork and allow to cool.

Mix the 1½ cups (375 mL) warm water and sugar in a large bowl. Stir in the oil, salt and yeast. Mix in the egg and cooked quinoa. Blend in the flour, starting with 3½ cups (875 mL). Work in another ¼ cup (60 mL) of flour. Grab the dough with a clean, dry hand to test stickiness. (If the dough sticks to your hand but pulls off, you have enough flour in the dough. If the dough remains stuck to your hand, add more flour.) Continue adding small amounts of flour, doing the "sticky test" after each addition (you should not require more than 4 cups/1 L of flour in total). Freeze unused portions of the dough in resealable freezer bags for up to 3 months.

Slice the dough in half for 2 large crusts or roll it into a log and cut it into 3 pieces for medium crusts. Form the pieces of dough into balls. Place the dough in a bowl that has been lightly sprayed with cooking oil or greased and cover with a clean kitchen towel. Place in a warm area to sit for about 15 minutes.

Preheat the oven to 425°F (220°C). Lightly grease the pizza pan(s) and press the dough evenly into each pan. Decorate with your favorite pizza sauce and toppings and bake on the center oven rack for 25 to 30 minutes (time may vary with different pizza pans and amount of toppings). Remove the pizza from the oven when the cheese in the center is bubbling and the bottom of the crust is golden brown. Refrigerate leftovers for up to 3 days.

To prepare leftover frozen dough, thaw overnight in the refrigerator. Place the dough in a bowl that has been lightly sprayed with cooking oil or grease, cover it with a dishcloth and allow the dough to rise as above.

The Perfect Baked Potato

Long consigned to side-dish status, the baked potato now has a chance to be the main attraction. Broccoli, bacon, red quinoa and aged cheddar cheese take a simple potato to a new level. Leave out the bacon to make a vegetarian or gluten-free version.

4 medium baking potatoes
1 tsp (5 mL) extra virgin olive oil
6 Tbsp (90 mL) water
3 Tbsp (45 mL) red quinoa
1 cup (250 mL) milk
¼ cup (60 mL) butter, melted
Salt to taste
2½ cups (625 mL) broccoli florets, steamed for 8 minutes and finely chopped

1½ cups (375 mL) shredded aged cheddar cheese
¾ cup (185 mL) chopped cooked bacon (optional)
¼ cup (60 mL) thinly sliced green onion
Light sour cream (optional)

Preheat the oven to 400°F (200°C). Wash and dry the potatoes, and then lightly brush them with olive oil. Bake on the center oven rack for 50 to 60 minutes, until they are soft.

While the potatoes bake, bring the water and quinoa to a boil in a small saucepan. Reduce to a simmer, cover and cook for 10 minutes. Turn the heat off and leave the covered saucepan on the burner for an additional 6 minutes. Fluff with a fork and set aside.

Heat the milk on the stove or in the microwave until hot. Remove the potatoes from the oven and make a lengthwise opening on each one. Use an oven mitt to hold the potato firmly, and gently scoop out the potato flesh. Set the potato skins aside and place the potato flesh in a large bowl. Mash the potato. Add the hot milk, butter and salt and blend until smooth and free of lumps. Stir in the broccoli, 1 cup (250 mL) of the cheddar cheese, the quinoa and the bacon (if using).

Gently scoop the potato mixture back into the potato skins. Top the stuffed potatoes with the remaining ½ cup (125 mL) cheddar cheese and the green onion. Return to the oven and bake for an additional 8 to 10 minutes, until the potato is warm and the cheese is bubbly. Serve with sour cream (if using).

Chapter 5

EVERYDAY TREATS

Cookies, Muffins & More

Do bakery delights with nutritious ingredi-ents sound like blasphemy? These mouth-watering recipes will transform your daily coffee break or teatime from sinful to saintly. We've transformed favorites such as cookies and brownies and basics like muffins and bread. If you want to make these recipes gluten-free, be sure ingredients such as oats and baking powder are labeled gluten-free.

Makes 12.

Raisin Bran Muffins

These moist, low-fat, high-fiber muffins are even better than Grandma's!

½ cup (125 mL) packed brown
    sugar
¼ cup (60 mL) cooking oil
¼ cup (60 mL) fancy molasses
2 large eggs
1 cup (250 mL) buttermilk or sour
    milk (see note page 23)

1½ cups (375 mL) wheat bran
½ cup (125 mL) quinoa flour
½ cup (125 mL) whole wheat flour
1½ tsp (7.5 mL) baking powder
¾ tsp (4 mL) salt
¼ tsp (1 mL) baking soda
½ cup (125 mL) raisins

Preheat the oven to 425°F (220°C). Line a 12-cup muffin pan with paper liners.

Measure the sugar and oil into a large bowl and mix until smooth. Beat in the molasses and eggs. Stir in the buttermilk, then the bran and set aside.

Combine the quinoa and whole wheat flours, baking powder, salt and baking soda in a medium bowl. Mix well and blend in the raisins.

Carefully fold the flour mixture into the molasses mixture, stirring just enough to blend but not overmix. Spoon the mixture evenly into the muffin cups.

Bake on the center oven rack for 18 to 20 minutes, until a toothpick inserted in the center of a muffin comes out clean.

Carrot Spice Muffins

These satisfying and light muffins are moist, with a hint of sweetness and spice. No butter or oil! If you want the decadent version, top with your favorite cream cheese frosting.

1⅓ cups (330 mL) quinoa flour
1 tsp (5 mL) baking powder
½ tsp (2 mL) baking soda
½ tsp (2 mL) salt
1½ tsp (7.5 mL) ground cinnamon
⅔ cup (160 mL) raisins
  (or ⅓ cup/80 mL raisins and
  ⅓ cup/80 mL chopped walnuts
  or pecans)

2 large eggs
½ cup (125 mL) packed brown
  sugar
⅔ cup (160 mL) plain yogurt
2¼ cups (560 mL) grated carrots

Preheat the oven to 350°F (180°C). Lightly spray a 12-cup muffin pan with cooking oil.

Combine the flour, baking powder, baking soda, salt and cinnamon in a medium bowl. Stir until well blended. Mix in the raisins and walnuts (if using) and set aside.

Whisk the eggs, sugar and yogurt in a large bowl. Stir in the grated carrots.

Using a spatula, gently stir the flour mixture into the carrot mixture until just blended. Scoop the batter evenly into the muffin cups. Bake on the center oven rack for 20 to 24 minutes, until a toothpick inserted in the center of a muffin comes out clean.

Remove the muffins from the oven and allow them to cool completely before removing them from the pan. Store in a sealed container in the refrigerator for up to 1 week or freeze for up to 1 month.

Raspberry Cream Cheese Muffins

The pleasing combination of raspberries and cream cheese with quinoa and whole wheat flour makes this a great snack you can feel good about eating.

½ cup (125 mL) white or golden quinoa

1 cup (250 mL) water

1¼ cups (310 mL) whole wheat flour

1½ tsp (7.5 mL) baking powder

¾ tsp (4 mL) salt

½ tsp (2 mL) ground cinnamon

¼ tsp (1 mL) baking soda

4 oz (114 mL) cold light cream cheese, diced small

1 cup (250 mL) frozen raspberries

¾ cup (185 mL) white or cane sugar

¼ cup (60 mL) vegetable oil

1 large egg

½ cup (125 mL) light sour cream

1 tsp (5 mL) pure vanilla extract

Bring the quinoa and water to a boil in a medium saucepan. Cover, reduce to a simmer and cook for 10 minutes. Turn the heat off and leave the covered saucepan on the burner for another 15 minutes. Fluff with a fork and allow the quinoa to cool.

Preheat the oven to 400°F (200°C). Line a 12-cup muffin pan with paper liners. Combine the flour, baking powder, salt, cinnamon and baking soda in a medium bowl and blend well. Add 1¼ cups (310 mL) of the cooked quinoa and mix until it is evenly coated with the flour mixture. Stir in the cream cheese, breaking up any large pieces. The cream cheese should remain chunky in these muffins. Add the frozen raspberries and coat in the flour mixture. Set aside.

In a large bowl, whisk together the sugar and oil, followed by the egg. Whisk in the sour cream and vanilla. Fold the flour mixture into the sugar mixture until just combined. Spoon the dough evenly among the cups. Bake on the center rack for 25 to 27 minutes, until the muffins are light brown around the edges and a toothpick inserted in the center of a muffin comes out clean. Store in a sealed container in the refrigerator for up to 1 week.

Makes 12.

Berry Flax Bran Muffins

Store-bought muffins can contain excessive amounts of fat. These muffins are easy to make, super healthy and truly enjoyable to eat.

½ cup (125 mL) packed brown sugar

¼ cup (60 mL) cooking oil

¼ cup (60 mL) fancy molasses

2 large eggs, beaten

1 cup (250 mL) buttermilk or sour milk (see note page 23)

¼ cup (60 mL) flax (ground or whole seeds)

1¼ cups (310 mL) wheat bran

½ cup (125 mL) quinoa flour

½ cup (125 mL) whole wheat flour

1½ tsp (7.5 mL) baking powder

¾ tsp (4 mL) salt

½ tsp (2 mL) baking soda

1 cup (250 mL) frozen raspberries or blueberries

Preheat the oven to 425°F (220°C). Line a 12-cup muffin pan with paper liners.

Measure the sugar and oil into a large bowl and blend together until smooth. Add the molasses and beaten eggs and mix thoroughly. Stir in the buttermilk, then the flax and bran. Set the mixture aside.

Combine the quinoa and whole wheat flours, baking powder, salt and baking soda in a medium bowl. Gently toss the berries into the dry mixture.

Carefully fold the flour mixture into the molasses mixture; stir just enough to blend but do not overmix.

Place large spoonfuls of the batter into the muffin cups, distributing it evenly.

Bake on the center oven rack for 16 to 20 minutes, or until a toothpick inserted in the center of a muffin comes out clean. Cool for a few minutes in the pan before removing from the pan and cooling completely on a rack. Store in a sealed container in the refrigerator for 1 week or in the freezer for up to 4 weeks.

Makes 12.

Lemon Blueberry Muffins

Cooked quinoa and whole wheat flour give hearty substance to these muffins. Blueberries and fresh lemon give them their flavor.

½ cup (125 mL) white or golden
    quinoa
1 cup (250 mL) water
1¼ cups (310 mL) whole wheat
    flour
1½ tsp (7.5 mL) baking powder
1 tsp (5 mL) salt
¼ tsp (1 mL) ground cinnamon
1 Tbsp (15 mL) grated lemon zest
    (about 1 lemon)

¾ cup (185 mL) white or cane
    sugar
¼ cup (60 mL) vegetable oil
½ cup (125 mL) sour cream
1 large egg
3 Tbsp (45 mL) fresh lemon juice
1 tsp (5 mL) pure vanilla extract
1 cup (250 mL) frozen blueberries
    (not thawed)

Bring the quinoa and water to a boil in a small saucepan. Reduce to a simmer, cover and cook for 10 minutes. Turn the heat off and leave the covered saucepan on the burner for an additional 15 minutes to allow the quinoa to cook longer and become plumper. Remove the lid and fluff with a fork. Set aside to cool.

Preheat the oven to 400°F (200°C). Line a 12-cup muffin pan with paper liners.

Combine the flour, baking powder, salt and cinnamon in a medium bowl. Stir in the lemon zest and 1¼ cups (310 mL) of the cooked quinoa, breaking up any clumps.

Whisk the sugar and oil in a large bowl, then add the sour cream, egg, lemon juice and vanilla. Stir until the mixture is thoroughly blended.

Toss the frozen blueberries in the flour mixture. Fold the flour mixture into the sugar mixture. Drop the batter by large spoonfuls into the muffin cups. Bake on the center oven rack for 25 to 30 minutes, until the tops are slightly golden and a toothpick inserted in the center comes out clean. Cool in the pan.

Makes 12.

Strawberry Banana Muffins

Strawberries and bananas make these muffins moist and full of wholesome goodness.

¼ cup (60 mL) white or golden quinoa

½ cup (125 mL) water

1 cup (250 mL) whole wheat flour

1½ tsp (7.5 mL) baking powder

1 tsp (5 mL) salt

1 tsp (5 mL) ground cinnamon

¾ cup (185 mL) packed brown sugar

¼ cup (60 mL) vegetable oil

½ cup (125 mL) plain yogurt or light sour cream

1 large egg

1 tsp (5 mL) pure vanilla extract

1 cup (250 mL) mashed ripe banana

1 cup (250 mL) diced frozen strawberries

Preheat the oven to 400°F (200°C). Line a 12-cup muffin pan with paper liners.

Bring the quinoa and water to a boil in a medium saucepan. Cover, reduce to a simmer and cook for 10 minutes. Turn the heat off and leave the covered saucepan on the burner for another 15 minutes. Fluff with a fork and allow the quinoa to cool.

Combine the flour, baking powder, salt and cinnamon in a medium bowl. Add the cooked quinoa to the flour mixture and blend well. Set aside.

Combine the sugar and oil in a large bowl. Mix in the yogurt, egg, vanilla and ripe banana.

Stir the frozen strawberries into the flour mixture. Gently stir the flour mixture into the banana mixture until just blended, being careful not to overmix. Use a large spoon to divide the batter evenly among the muffin cups. Bake on the center oven rack for 28 to 30 minutes or until a toothpick inserted in the center of a muffin comes out clean. Cool in the pan. Refrigerate leftovers in a sealed container or freeze for up to 1 month.

Makes 5 dozen.

Healthy Cookies

This is one healthy cookie, and a great snack to keep you going until your next meal.

⅔ cup (160 mL) water
⅓ cup (80 mL) quinoa
1 cup (250 mL) butter, softened
1⅓ cups (330 mL) packed brown
    sugar
2 large eggs
1½ tsp (7.5 mL) pure vanilla
    extract
2 cups (500 mL) whole wheat flour
1½ tsp (7.5 mL) baking powder
1 tsp (5 mL) baking soda

1 tsp (5 mL) ground cinnamon
¼ tsp (1 mL) salt
1¼ cups (310 mL) quick-cooking
    rolled oats
1 cup (250 mL) flaked
    unsweetened coconut
⅓ cup (80 mL) sunflower seeds,
    unsalted
⅓ cup (80 mL) flax (ground or
    whole seeds)
⅓ cup (80 mL) sesame seeds

Bring the water and quinoa to a boil in a small saucepan. Reduce to a simmer, cover and cook for 10 minutes. Turn the heat off and leave the covered saucepan on the burner for an additional 6 minutes. Remove the lid and fluff with a fork. Set aside to cool.

Preheat the oven to 350°F (180°C).

Cream the butter with the brown sugar in a large bowl. Add the eggs and vanilla and mix thoroughly.

Combine the flour, baking powder, baking soda, cinnamon and salt in a medium bowl. Add the oats, cooked quinoa, coconut, sunflower seeds, flax and sesame seeds to the flour mixture and stir until well blended. Combine with the butter mixture and stir until well mixed. Roll the dough into 1½-inch (4 cm) balls. Place 2 inches (5 cm) apart on a baking sheet. Flatten each cookie slightly with the palm of your hand. Bake on the center oven rack for 8 to 10 minutes, until the bottoms are light brown. Allow the cookies to cool completely on the baking sheet. Store the cookies in a sealed container in the refrigerator for up to 1 week.

Quinoa Shortbread

This shortbread has the nutritious advantage of quinoa but still has that melt-in-your-mouth goodness. These cookies look great decorated for the holidays. An easy method for shaping the cookies is to form the dough into a log, chill it in the refrigerator and slice perfect rounds.

1 cup (250 mL) all-purpose flour
¾ cup (185 mL) quinoa flour
1 cup (250 mL) butter
1 cup (250 mL) superfine sugar (or
    white sugar)

¼ cup (60 mL) chocolate chunks
    or chocolate chips

Preheat the oven to 500°F (260°C).

Sift the flours together and evenly spread the mixture onto a large baking sheet. Place on the top oven rack for 4 to 5 minutes, until the flour has a lightly toasted appearance. Remove the pan from the oven, gently stir the flour and toast for another 4 to 5 minutes.

Remove from the oven and let cool for 1 to 2 minutes. Sift the flour into a large bowl. Reduce the oven temperature to 350°F (180°C).

Cream the butter and sugar in a separate bowl. Slowly add the flour, mixing well. Chill the dough in the refrigerator for at least 20 minutes.

Roll the dough into 2-inch (5 cm) balls and place them at least 2 inches (5 cm) apart on a large baking sheet. Gently press a small chocolate chunk (or several chocolate chips) into the middle of each cookie.

Place on the center rack of the oven and bake for 18 to 20 minutes.

Remove from the oven and cool on the baking sheet for 10 to 15 minutes. Store the cookies in a sealed container in the refrigerator for up to 2 weeks.

Makes 3 dozen.

Double Chocolate Cookies

The recipe for these absolutely delicious, chewy and soft cookies was a closely guarded secret for years! Guaranteed they will not last long! (Pictured on page 142.)

1 cup (250 mL) butter, softened
1½ cups (375 mL) white or cane
    sugar
2 large eggs
1 tsp (5 mL) pure vanilla extract
2 cups (500 mL) quinoa flour (or
    1 cup/250 mL quinoa flour and
    1 cup/250 mL all-purpose flour)

¾ cup (185 mL) unsweetened
    cocoa powder
1 tsp (5 mL) baking soda
½ tsp (2 mL) salt
1 cup (250 mL) semisweet
    chocolate chips

Preheat the oven to 350°F (180°C).

Cream the butter and sugar in a large bowl. Blend in the eggs and vanilla and stir until the mixture has a smooth consistency.

In a separate bowl, combine the flour, cocoa, baking soda and salt. Add the flour mixture to the butter mixture and blend well. Stir in the chocolate chips. Roll into 1¼-inch (3 cm) balls. (If the dough is too soft to roll, place in the freezer for about 20 minutes.)

Place the balls 2 inches (5 cm) apart on a large, ungreased baking sheet and flatten slightly with the palm of your hand. Bake on the center oven rack for 8 to 10 minutes. The cookies will be puffy and soft when removed from the oven but will flatten when cool. Allow the cookies to set for at least 1 minute on the baking sheet before removing to cool on a rack. Store in a sealed container for up to 1 week or freeze for up to 1 month. You can also freeze rolled unbaked cookies in a sealed container or plastic bag until needed; simply thaw before baking.

White Chocolate Macadamia Nut Cookies

Speedy and easy! The smooth taste of macadamia nuts with white chocolate is a popular cookie combination.

½ cup (125 mL) quinoa flour

½ cup (125 mL) all-purpose flour

¼ tsp (1 mL) baking soda

½ cup (125 mL) packed brown
  sugar

½ cup (125 mL) butter, softened

1 large egg

½ tsp (2 mL) pure vanilla extract

1 cup (250 mL) white chocolate
  chunks

¾ cup (185 mL) coarsely chopped
  macadamia nuts

Preheat the oven to 350°F (180°C).

In a medium bowl, combine the quinoa and all-purpose flours with the baking soda.

In a separate bowl, cream the sugar and butter. Beat in the egg and vanilla, combining well. Add the flour mixture to the butter mixture and blend well. Add the chocolate and nuts and mix well. Drop by 2-inch (5 cm) tablespoonfuls onto ungreased baking sheets, leaving 2 inches (5 cm) between cookies. Bake on the center oven rack for 12 minutes. Cool on the pan and serve. Store leftovers in a sealed container in the refrigerator for up to 1 week or freeze them for up to 6 weeks.

Makes 2 dozen.

Chocolate Sugar Cookies

Homemade sugar cookies are a seasonal favorite in many families and can be decorated for any season. In a sealed container, these cookies will stay fresh for up to ten days in the refrigerator or eight weeks in the freezer.

⅔ cup (160 mL) butter, softened

2 large eggs

1 cup (250 mL) sugar

⅓ cup (80 mL) unsweetened cocoa powder

⅓ cup (80 mL) milk

1 tsp (5 mL) pure vanilla extract

1⅓ cups (330 mL) all-purpose flour

1⅓ cups (330 mL) quinoa flour

1 Tbsp (15 mL) baking powder

½ tsp (2 mL) salt

Beat the butter, eggs, sugar and cocoa powder together in a medium bowl with an electric mixer. Add the milk and vanilla extract and continue to mix until well blended.

In a separate bowl, combine both flours, the baking powder and salt.

Add the butter mixture to the flour mixture and blend well. Form the dough into a large ball and chill in the refrigerator for 1 hour.

Preheat the oven to 350°F (180°C). Lightly grease a large baking sheet or line with parchment paper.

On a lightly floured surface, roll the dough to a thickness of about ¼ inch (6 mm). Cut shapes using lightly floured cookie cutters. Using a metal baking spatula, carefully transfer the cookies to the baking sheet, placing at least 1 inch (2.5 cm) apart. Bake for 8 to 10 minutes, remove from the oven and cool on the pan for 5 minutes before moving to a rack to cool completely. Decorate with chocolate hazelnut spread, jam or frosting, if desired.

Makes 3 dozen.

Chewy Chocolate Chip Cookies

If you think chocolate chip cookies couldn't possibly be healthy, try these (pictured on page 142). Quinoa flour makes these cookies chewy and scrumptious. Store them in a sealed container for up to two weeks. For last-minute cookies, keep a batch of prerolled unbaked cookies in your freezer for up to one month.

2¼ cups (560 mL) quinoa flour (or
    1¼ cups/310 mL quinoa flour
    and 1 cup/250 mL all-purpose
    flour)
½ tsp (2 mL) baking soda
1 cup (250 mL) butter, softened
¾ cup (185 mL) white or cane
    sugar

¾ cup (185 mL) packed brown
    sugar
1 tsp (5 mL) salt
2 tsp (10 mL) pure vanilla extract
2 large eggs
1½ cups (375 mL) semisweet
    chocolate chips

Preheat the oven to 350°F (180°C). Grease a large baking sheet or line with parchment paper.

Mix the flour and baking soda in a small bowl and set aside.

In a large bowl, blend the butter and sugars until smooth and fluffy. Add the salt, vanilla and eggs and mix until well blended. Stir in the flour mixture and blend well. Mix in the chocolate chips.

Roll the dough into 1-inch (2.5 cm) balls and place 2 inches (5 cm) apart on the baking sheet.

Bake on the center oven rack for 8 to 10 minutes. The cookies will be puffy and soft when removed from the oven, but will flatten when cooled. Allow the cookies to sit for 1 minute before removing from the pan to a rack to cool completely. Store in a sealed container in the refrigerator for up to 1 week or freeze for up to 1 month.

Chocolate Almond Biscotti

Enjoy your coffee break with these perfectly dippable biscotti. Bundled in a clear bag trimmed with ribbons, they make an attractive and wholesome gift.

1½ cups (375 mL) slivered almonds

1½ cups (375 mL) quinoa flour

½ cup (125 mL) whole wheat flour

½ cup (125 mL) unsweetened cocoa powder

½ tsp (2 mL) baking powder

½ tsp (2 mL) baking soda

¼ tsp (1 mL) salt

½ cup (125 mL) mini semisweet chocolate chips (optional)

¼ cup (60 mL) softened butter

1 cup (250 mL) white or cane sugar

3 large eggs

1 tsp (5 mL) pure vanilla extract

1 tsp (5 mL) almond extract

Preheat the oven to 350°F (180°C).

Place the slivered almonds on a baking sheet in a single layer and toast on the top oven rack for 6 to 8 minutes, until golden and fragrant. Remove from the oven and let cool.

Combine the quinoa and whole wheat flours, cocoa, baking powder, baking soda and salt in a large bowl. Gently stir in the cooled almonds and chocolate chips (if using).

Cream together the butter and sugar in a medium bowl. Add the eggs, vanilla and almond extract and blend well.

Lightly spray a baking sheet with cooking oil or grease, or line with parchment paper. Divide the dough in half and roll it into long logs that are the same length as the baking sheet. Dampen your hands and lightly pat the dough to flatten it to a ¾-inch (2 cm) thickness. Repeat with the other half of the dough. Place both pieces of dough on the baking sheet and bake on the center oven rack for 20 minutes.

Remove from the oven and let sit until cool enough to touch. Slice each log into 1-inch (2.5 cm) pieces. Place the slices on the same baking sheet and bake an additional 6 minutes on each side. Remove from the oven and cool. Store in a sealed bag or container for up to 8 weeks.

Pecan Chocolate Oatmeal Cookies

Ground oats give these cookies a smoother texture, making them a unique alterna-tive to the regular oatmeal cookie. Pecans and chocolate make them decadent.

2½ cups (625 mL) large-flake
    rolled oats
1 cup (250 mL) quinoa flour
1 cup (250 mL) whole wheat flour
1 tsp (5 mL) baking soda
1 tsp (5 mL) baking powder
½ tsp (2 mL) salt
1 cup (250 mL) butter, softened
1 cup (250 mL) packed brown
    sugar

2 large eggs
¼ cup (60 mL) plain yogurt
1 tsp (5 mL) pure vanilla extract
1½ cups (375 mL) semisweet
    chocolate chips
1½ cups (375 mL) coarsely
    chopped pecans

Preheat the oven to 375°F (190°C).

Process the oats in a blender or food processor until finely ground. Transfer to a large bowl and add the quinoa flour, whole wheat flour, baking soda, baking powder and salt. Mix well.

Combine the butter, sugar, eggs, yogurt and vanilla in a medium bowl, mixing well. Add the oat mixture to the butter mixture and mix well. Stir in the chocolate chips and pecans.

If the dough is too sticky to work with, chill in the refrigerator for 20 minutes. Roll the dough into 2-inch (5 cm) balls and place at least 2 inches (5 cm) apart on a large baking sheet. Press with a fork to slightly flatten them. Bake on the center oven rack for 12 to 14 minutes, until the edges are lightly golden. To keep the cookies moist and chewy, do not overbake. Cool completely on the baking sheet. Store in a sealed con-tainer in the refrigerator for up to 1 week or freeze for up to 1 month.

Makes 3 dozen.

Oatmeal Raisin Cookies

This is an even healthier version of a longtime favorite. The dough can be rolled into balls and frozen for up to four weeks, allowing you to quickly pop them in the oven and serve fresh-baked cookies to last-minute guests. If you wish to make them gluten-free, ensure you use gluten-free ingredients.

3 cups (750 mL) large-flake rolled oats
1½ cups (375 mL) quinoa flour (or ¾ cup/185 mL quinoa flour and ¾ cup/185 mL all-purpose flour)
½ tsp (2 mL) salt
1 tsp (5 mL) baking soda
2 tsp (10 mL) ground cinnamon

½ tsp (2 mL) ground cloves
¼ cup (60 mL) white sugar
1 cup (250 mL) packed brown sugar
1 cup (250 mL) butter, softened
2 large eggs
1 tsp (5 mL) pure vanilla extract
1½ cups (375 mL) raisins

Preheat the oven to 350°F (180°C). Grease a baking sheet or line with parchment paper. Measure the oats, flour, salt, baking soda, cinnamon and cloves into a large bowl. In a separate bowl, cream both the sugars and the butter together. Add the eggs and vanilla and mix well. Add the butter mixture to the oat mixture and blend until a soft dough forms. Stir in the raisins.

Roll the dough into 1½-inch (4 cm) balls and flatten to a thickness of ½ inch (1 cm) with the palm of your hand. Place them 2 inches (5 cm) apart on the baking sheet. Bake on the center oven rack for 10 to 12 minutes, until the edges are golden brown. Remove from the oven and cool the cookies for 1 minute before removing them to cool completely on a rack. Store in a sealed container in the refrigerator for up to 1 week.

Clockwise, from right:
Ginger Molasses Cookies (facing page),
Double Chocolate Cookies (page 134) and
Chewy Chocolate Chip Cookies (page 138).

Makes 3 dozen.

Ginger Molasses Cookies

A modern twist on grandma's favorite cookie. For a chewy, soft cookie, make as directed. If you enjoy a crisper cookie, bake for an additional two to four minutes.

½ cup (125 mL) butter
1 cup (250 mL) packed brown
  sugar
1 large egg
¼ cup (60 mL) fancy molasses
2 cups (500 mL) quinoa flour (or
  1 cup/250 mL quinoa flour and
  1 cup/250 mL all-purpose flour)

2 tsp (10 mL) baking soda
½ tsp (2 mL) salt
1 tsp (5 mL) ground ginger
2 tsp (10 mL) ground cinnamon
½ tsp (2 mL) ground cloves
¼ cup (60 mL) white sugar

Preheat the oven to 350°F (180°C). Cream the butter and brown sugar in a large bowl. Beat in the egg and molasses. Set aside.

Mix the flour, baking soda, salt, ginger, cinnamon and cloves in a medium bowl and blend well. Add the butter mixture to the flour mixture and mix until a smooth dough forms.

Roll the dough into 1½-inch (4 cm) balls. Place the white sugar in a shallow bowl and roll each ball to coat. Place 2 inches (5 cm) apart on a baking sheet and bake on the center oven rack for 8 to 10 minutes. The cookies should be puffy and slightly browned on the bottom when you remove them from the pan. Let them cool for 1 minute to set before removing them to cool completely on a rack.

Store for 1 week in a sealed container in the refrigerator or 4 weeks in the freezer.

Makes 2 dozen.

Peanut Butter Cookies

The flavor of peanut butter perfectly complements quinoa flour. These buttery, crisp cookies are great with a tall glass of cold milk.

2 cups (500 mL) quinoa flour (or
   1 cup/250 mL quinoa flour and
   1 cup/250 mL all-purpose flour)
2 tsp (10 mL) baking soda
¼ tsp (1 mL) salt
1 cup (250 mL) butter

¾ cup (185 mL) white sugar
¾ cup (185 mL) packed brown
   sugar
2 large eggs
1½ cups (375 mL) peanut butter

Preheat the oven to 375°F (190°C).

Combine the flour, baking soda and salt in a medium bowl and set aside.

Cream the butter with both sugars until smooth. Beat in the eggs and add the peanut butter, mixing well. Gradually add the flour mixture and blend well. Chill the dough in the refrigerator for 20 minutes.

Roll the dough into 1-inch (2.5 cm) balls and place 2 inches (5 cm) apart on an ungreased baking sheet. Flatten the balls with a fork in a crisscross design.

Place on the center oven rack and bake for 8 to 10 minutes, until the cookies brown slightly on the edges and puff up.

Remove the cookies from the oven and cool for 1 minute on the pan before transferring to a rack to cool. Store in a sealed container in the refrigerator for up to 1 week.

Makes 16.

Toffee Mocha Squares

These small melt-in-your-mouth bites of chocolate, buttery toffee and rich mocha are perfect paired with a cup of coffee.

⅓ cup (80 mL) chopped pecans

⅓ cup (80 mL) butter, softened

½ cup (125 mL) packed brown sugar

1 large egg

2 tsp (10 mL) strong coffee or 1 tsp (5 mL) coffee liqueur

1 cup (250 mL) quinoa flour

1 cup (250 mL) toffee bits

¼ tsp (1 mL) baking soda

Pinch salt

1 cup (250 mL) semisweet chocolate chips

Preheat the oven to 350°F (180°C). Spread the pecans evenly on a baking sheet and bake on the center oven rack for 5 to 7 minutes, until they are fragrant and lightly toasted. Remove from the oven and set aside.

Grease a 9-inch (23 cm) square baking pan and line the bottom with parchment paper.

Cream the butter and sugar in a medium bowl until smooth. Mix in the egg and coffee. Add the quinoa flour, toffee bits, baking soda and salt. Mix thoroughly and press into the baking dish. Bake on the center oven rack for 15 minutes or until lightly golden.

Remove from the oven and sprinkle evenly with the chocolate chips. Return to the oven for 1 more minute. Using a butter knife, spread the melted chocolate chips evenly across the baked dough. Sprinkle immediately with the toasted pecans. Cool completely before cutting into 16 squares. Store leftovers in a sealed container in the refrigerator for up to 1 week or in the freezer for up to 1 month.

Makes 16.

Chocolate Cheesecake Brownies

Indulgence with a touch of wholesomeness. These brownies will keep for up to one week in a sealed container in the refrigerator or will freeze for up to eight weeks.

Brownie base		
1½ cups (375 mL) semisweet chocolate chips	2 large eggs	
½ cup (125 mL) butter	½ tsp (2 mL) pure vanilla extract	
⅓ cup (80 mL) sugar	½ cup (125 mL) quinoa flour	

Brownie base

1½ cups (375 mL) semisweet
   chocolate chips
½ cup (125 mL) butter
⅓ cup (80 mL) sugar

2 large eggs
½ tsp (2 mL) pure vanilla extract
½ cup (125 mL) quinoa flour

Cheesecake topping

One 8 oz (250 g) package light
   cream cheese, softened
½ tsp (2 mL) pure vanilla extract
¼ cup (60 mL) sugar
1 large egg

1 Tbsp (15 mL) milk
2 Tbsp (30 mL) quinoa flour
¼ cup (60 mL) semisweet
   chocolate chips

Preheat the oven to 325°F (160°C). Spray or grease a 9-inch (23 cm) square baking pan and line with parchment paper.

In a small saucepan over low heat, melt the chocolate chips and butter together. Stir the mixture until smooth and remove from the heat. Set aside to cool.

In a medium bowl, beat the sugar, eggs and vanilla with an electric mixer. Add the melted chocolate and mix well. Add the flour and mix until thoroughly blended. Spread evenly in the bottom of the baking pan.

In a medium bowl, beat the cream cheese, vanilla, sugar and egg together with an electric mixer. Blend in the milk and flour. Divide the cheesecake mixture in half and set half aside. Spread the other half evenly over the brownie base in the pan.

In a small saucepan over medium-low heat, melt the chocolate chips. When the chocolate is smooth, remove from the heat and cool slightly. Add to the reserved cheesecake mixture and blend well. Drizzle this mixture over the plain cheesecake mixture in the pan. Swirl the surface of the cheesecake with a knife until the desired pattern is achieved.

Bake on the center oven rack for 30 to 35 minutes, until the middle of the cheesecake springs back when gently pressed. Cool and chill before cutting into 16 squares. Serve chilled.

Chocolate Truffle Brownies

For brownie connoisseurs, this is a classic brownie with an unusual trufflelike texture that is a perfect balance between a fudgy brownie and a cakey brownie. Store brownies for up to one week in a sealed container in the refrigerator.

4 oz (115 g) unsweetened
    chocolate (4 squares)
¾ cup (185 mL) butter
1½ cups (375 mL) sugar
3 large eggs

2 tsp (10 mL) pure vanilla extract
1¼ cups (310 mL) quinoa flour
¼ cup (60 mL) milk
1 cup (250 mL) chopped pecans or
    walnuts

Preheat the oven to 350°F (180°C). Lightly spray or grease a 9-inch (23 cm) square baking pan and lightly sprinkle with flour or line with parchment paper.

In a small saucepan, melt the chocolate and the butter together over low heat. Add the sugar, stirring constantly. When the mixture is thoroughly blended, pour into a large bowl. Add the eggs and vanilla to the chocolate mixture and blend well. Stir in the flour and milk. Mix in the nuts. Pour evenly into the baking pan.

Bake on the center oven rack for 20 to 22 minutes. To keep these brownies chewy, be careful not to overbake. Cool for 15 minutes in the pan before cutting into 16 squares.

Date Squares

Matrimonial cake made thick and full of dates. This cake is gluten-free when made with oats processed in a gluten-free facility. Store for up to one week in the refrigerator or freeze for up to two months.

2 cups (500 mL) chopped, pitted dates
¾ cup (185 mL) boiling water
1 tsp (5 mL) fresh lemon juice
2¼ cups (560 mL) quinoa flour
2¼ cups (560 mL) large-flake rolled oats

¾ cup (185 mL) packed brown sugar
Pinch salt
1½ cups (375 mL) butter, softened

Preheat the oven to 375°F (190°C). Grease a 9-inch (23 cm) square baking pan or spray with cooking oil.

In a small saucepan over medium heat, combine the dates and boiling water. Stir until the water has been absorbed and the dates are smooth. Remove from the heat and stir in the lemon juice. Set aside.

Combine the flour, oats, sugar, salt and butter to make a crumbly mixture. Divide into 2 portions and press one-half firmly into the pan to make a base. Spread the date mixture evenly on top. Add the remaining crumb mixture to the top, lightly pressing it down with your hands. Bake on the center oven rack for 25 minutes. Remove from the oven and allow to completely cool in the pan. Chill, cut into 16 squares and serve.

Raspberry Coconut Bars

A delicately sweet treat that is great for entertaining or special occasions.

Crust

¾ cup (185 mL) packed brown sugar
½ cup (125 mL) butter, softened

½ tsp (2 mL) almond extract
1 large egg, lightly beaten
1½ cups (375 mL) quinoa flour

Topping

1 cup (250 mL) raspberry jam or preserves
2 large eggs, lightly beaten

2 cups (500 mL) flaked unsweetened coconut

Preheat the oven to 350°F (180°C). Spray with cooking oil or grease a 9- × 13-inch (3.5 L) baking dish. Cut a piece of parchment paper to fit the bottom of the dish.

Combine the sugar, butter and almond extract in a medium bowl and blend well. Add the egg and mix until thoroughly combined. Add the quinoa flour and work into a soft dough. Press the dough evenly into the bottom of the baking dish. Spread the raspberry jam over the dough.

In a medium bowl, mix the eggs and coconut together and drop the mixture evenly over the jam. Place on the center rack of the oven and bake for 20 minutes or until the coconut is lightly toasted. Remove from the oven and cool in the pan for 1 hour before cutting into 16 bars. Store in a sealed container in the refrigerator for up to 1 week.

Maple Bean Tarts

You'd never guess these syrupy maple tarts are made with quinoa and beans! Quinoa pastry has a tan color and a nutty flavor that is perfect with sweet maple. This pastry won't fluff up as much as regular pastry and will be slightly more delicate, so take extra care when removing the tarts from the pan. Indulge by topping them with whipped cream. Store in a sealed container in the refrigerator for up to one week.

Pastry		
	1¼ cups (310 mL) quinoa flour	½ cup (125 mL) cold butter, cubed
	3 Tbsp (45 mL) white or cane sugar	1 Tbsp (15 mL) water

Filling		
	1 cup (250 mL) cooked navy beans	⅓ cup (80 mL) melted butter
	½ cup (125 mL) maple syrup	½ cup (125 mL) chopped pecans
	2 large eggs	12 pecan halves (optional)
	½ cup (125 mL) packed brown sugar	

Mix the flour and sugar in a large bowl. Cut the butter into the mixture until it resembles small crumbs. Add the water and use your hands to pat it into a soft dough. Refrigerate for 45 to 60 minutes.

Preheat the oven to 350°F (180°C). Grease a 12-cup muffin pan or spray with cooking oil. On a lightly floured surface, roll out the dough to a thickness of about ¼ inch (6 mm). Using a 3-inch (7.5 cm) round cookie cutter (or a large water glass), cut 12 circles. Gently press the dough into the tart pans.

Place the beans and maple syrup in a blender or food processor and purée until smooth. Continue blending while adding the eggs, brown sugar and butter. Add the chopped pecans and pulse 1 or 2 more times. Pour the mixture evenly into the tart shells. Garnish the top of each tart with a pecan (if using).

Bake on the center oven rack for 20 minutes. Cool completely in the pan before removing. Store in a sealed container in the refrigerator for up to 3 days.

Makes 1 loaf.

Irish Soda Bread

A quick and versatile bread that pairs well with any meal. Make this plain, choose one of the variations below or use your own favorite herbs to customize the loaf.

1 cup (250 mL) milk	¾ tsp (4 mL) baking soda
1 Tbsp (15 mL) fresh lemon juice	½ tsp (2 mL) salt
1 cup (250 mL) quinoa flour	3 Tbsp (45 mL) butter
1 cup (250 mL) whole wheat flour	½ tsp (2 mL) milk

Preheat the oven to 375°F (190°C). Grease a large baking sheet, spray with cooking oil or line with parchment paper.

Combine the 1 cup (250 mL) of milk and lemon juice in a small bowl. Set aside.

In a large bowl, combine the quinoa and whole wheat flours, baking soda and salt. Cut the butter into the flour mixture, making small pea-sized crumbs. Form a well with the dry ingredients and pour in the milk mixture. Starting from the center, blend the ingredients slowly until the mixture forms a soft dough.

With floured hands, remove the dough from the bowl to the center of the baking sheet. Form it into a large, round ball. Gently flatten the ball to about 2 inches (5 cm) in thickness and brush the surface with the ½ tsp (2 mL) of milk. Cut a large shallow X across the top of the bread using a sharp knife. Bake on the center oven rack for 30 to 35 minutes. Remove from the oven, allow to cool slightly on the baking sheet and cut into wedges. Serve warm.

Variations

Rosemary Parmesan Bread. Add 1 tsp (5 mL) rosemary and ½ cup (125 mL) grated Parmesan cheese to the flour mixture. (Great with soups or stews.)

Cheddar Cheese Bread. Add 1 cup (250 mL) shredded aged cheddar cheese after cutting in the butter, and sprinkle another ¼ cup (60 mL) on top of the loaf prior to baking.

Makes 20.

Herb Biscuits

The aroma of fresh herbs in these biscuits is an incentive to serve them the way they taste best—straight from the oven, with butter. Use a 3-inch (7.5 cm) cutter.

1 cup (250 mL) quinoa flour
1 cup (250 mL) whole wheat flour
1 Tbsp (15 mL) baking powder
1 tsp (5 mL) baking soda
¼ tsp (1 mL) salt
½ cup (125 mL) butter

¼ cup (60 mL) chopped fresh parsley
1 Tbsp (15 mL) chopped fresh dill
¾ cup (185 mL) buttermilk or sour milk (see note page 23)

Preheat the oven to 425°F (220°C).

In a large bowl, mix the quinoa and whole wheat flours, baking powder, baking soda and salt. Cut in the butter until the mixture is crumbly. Add the parsley and dill and mix well. Add the buttermilk and stir until well combined. Turn out the dough onto a floured surface and knead gently for a few minutes.

Pat or roll out the dough to a ½-inch (1 cm) thickness. Using a floured cookie cutter, cut shapes and place them on an ungreased baking sheet ½ inch (1 cm) apart.

Bake on the center oven rack for 10 to 12 minutes, until the biscuits are lightly browned. Remove them from the baking sheet to cool on a wire rack. Enjoy cold or reheat for 1 to 2 minutes in the oven or a toaster oven just before serving. Store the biscuits in a sealed container in the refrigerator for up to 2 days.

Chapter 6

EVERYDAY DESSERTS

Satisfy Your Sweet Tooth

Satisfy a sweet tooth with healthful ingredients? It can be done with quinoa. These recipes will please a variety of tastes, with everything from fruit to chocolate. Celebrate a special occasion, wow guests at your next dinner party or break up the routine of those regular family dinners with an unusual dessert. Make the Decadent Chocolate Mousse or Apple Cinnamon Cheesecake to please a crowd, or even just for yourself! If you want to make these recipes gluten-free, be sure to use gluten-free oats and baking powder.

Serves 8.

Apple Cinnamon Cheesecake

The nutty flavor of the quinoa crust with cream cheese and cinnamon-flavored apples makes this a home-baked delight. Garnish with vanilla ice cream, if desired.

Crust
1¼ cups (310 mL) quinoa flour
¼ cup (60 mL) white or cane sugar
1 tsp (5 mL) ground cinnamon
½ cup (125 mL) softened butter
1 Tbsp (15 mL) water

Filling
One 8 oz (250 g) package light cream cheese, softened
¼ cup (60 mL) white or cane sugar
1 large egg
1 Tbsp (15 mL) quinoa flour
2 tsp (10 mL) fresh lemon juice
½ tsp (2 mL) pure vanilla extract

Topping
2 Granny Smith apples, peeled and sliced in ¼-inch-thick (6 mm) pieces
2 Tbsp (30 mL) white or cane sugar
½ tsp (2 mL) ground cinnamon

Preheat the oven to 350°F (180°C). (If using a metal pan instead of a pie plate, bake at 325°F/160°C.) Grease a 9-inch (23 cm) round pie plate or lightly spray with cooking oil.

Combine the flour, sugar and cinnamon in a large bowl. Cut in the butter and use your fingers to make a soft crumble. Drizzle in the water and use your hands to form a soft dough. Press evenly into the pie plate and set aside.

Combine the cream cheese and sugar in a medium bowl. Add the egg, flour, lemon juice and vanilla. Blend with an electric mixer until thoroughly combined. Pour the filling into the crust and set aside.

Toss the sliced apples, sugar and cinnamon together in a medium bowl. Gently place them on top of the cheesecake filling. Place on the center oven rack and bake for 1 hour or until the apples are tender. If the crust or apples are becoming too dark, cover the cake with a piece of foil for the remaining baking time. Cool the cake completely before slicing into 8 pieces.

Apple Toffee Cake

Accompany this toffee cake with a hot cup of coffee and good conversation.

½ cup (125 mL) butter, softened
1 cup (250 mL) packed brown
  sugar
2 large eggs
1½ tsp (7.5 mL) pure vanilla
  extract
1 cup (250 mL) plain yogurt or sour
  cream
1 cup (250 mL) quinoa flour

1 cup (250 mL) whole wheat flour
1 tsp (5 mL) baking powder
1 tsp (5 mL) baking soda
¼ tsp (1 mL) salt
2 cups (500 mL) peeled and diced
  apples
1 bag (200 g) toffee bits
¾ tsp (4 mL) ground cinnamon

Preheat the oven to 350°F (180°C). Lightly grease a 9- × 13-inch (3.5 L) baking dish.

Beat the butter, ⅔ cup (160 mL) of the sugar, eggs and vanilla in a large bowl. Stir in the yogurt and set aside.

Combine the quinoa and whole wheat flours, baking powder, baking soda and salt in a medium bowl and mix well. Fold the flour mixture into the butter mixture. Fold the apples and toffee bits gently into the batter. Spread the batter evenly into the baking dish. Mix the remaining ⅓ cup (80 mL) of brown sugar and the cinnamon in a small bowl. Sprinkle the mixture over the top of the batter. Bake on the center oven rack for 30 to 35 minutes, or until a toothpick inserted in the center comes out clean. Cool in the pan before cutting into serving-size pieces. Store in a resealable container in the refrigerator for up to 2 days.

Serves 16.

Carrot Cake

Discouraged by the high-sugar, high-fat content of carrot cake? This recipe will satisfy your carrot cake craving without all of the empty calories.

Cake
- 2 cups (500 mL) quinoa flour
- 2½ tsp (12 mL) ground cinnamon
- 2 tsp (10 mL) baking powder
- 2 tsp (10 mL) baking soda
- ½ tsp (2 mL) salt
- ¼ tsp (1 mL) ground nutmeg
- 1 cup (250 mL) finely chopped pecans or walnuts
- 1 cup (250 mL) white or cane sugar
- ¾ cup (185 mL) vegetable oil
- 4 large eggs
- 1 cup (250 mL) unsweetened applesauce
- 2 tsp (10 mL) pure vanilla extract
- 3 cups (750 mL) grated carrots

Frosting
- One 8 oz (250 g) package light cream cheese, softened
- ⅓ cup (80 mL) butter, softened
- 2 tsp (10 mL) fresh lemon juice
- 1½ cups (375 mL) icing sugar
- ¼ cup (60 mL) finely chopped pecans or walnuts (optional)

Preheat the oven to 350°F (180°C). Lightly grease a 9- × 13-inch (3.5 L) baking pan or spray with cooking oil. Cut a piece of parchment paper to fit the bottom of the pan. This will make for easy removal of the cake.

Combine the flour, cinnamon, baking powder, baking soda, salt and nutmeg in a large bowl. Stir in the pecans. Set aside.

Whisk the sugar and oil in a medium bowl. Whisk in the eggs, apple-sauce and vanilla. Stir in the carrots.

Blend the egg mixture into the flour mixture until just combined. Pour into the pan and bake on the center oven rack for about 45 minutes or until a knife inserted in the center comes out clean. Set aside to cool completely to room temperature.

Beat the cream cheese and butter together in a large bowl with an electric mixer until light and fluffy. Gradually add the lemon juice and icing sugar until smooth and creamy.

Spread the frosting evenly over the top of the cake and sprinkle with the nuts. Cut into 16 portions and serve. Refrigerate leftovers for up to 1 week.

Serves 8–16.

Moist Chocolate Cake

No one will believe this chocolate cake is made with cooked quinoa—no flour required!

⅔ cup (160 mL) white or golden quinoa

1⅓ cups (330 mL) water

⅓ cup (80 mL) milk

4 large eggs

1 tsp (5 mL) pure vanilla extract

¾ cup (185 mL) butter, melted and cooled

1½ cups (375 mL) white or cane sugar

1 cup (250 mL) unsweetened cocoa powder

1½ tsp (7.5 mL) baking powder

½ tsp (2 mL) baking soda

½ tsp (2 mL) salt

Bring the quinoa and water to a boil in a medium saucepan. Cover, reduce to a simmer and cook for 10 minutes. Turn off the heat and leave the covered saucepan on the burner for another 10 minutes. Fluff with a fork and allow the quinoa to cool.

Preheat the oven to 350°F (180°C). Lightly grease two 8-inch (20 cm) round or square cake pans. Line the bottoms of the pans with parchment paper.

Combine the milk, eggs and vanilla in a blender or food processor. Add 2 cups (500 mL) of cooked quinoa and the butter and continue to blend until smooth.

Whisk together the sugar, cocoa, baking powder, baking soda and salt in a medium bowl. Add the contents of the blender and mix well. Divide the batter evenly between the 2 pans and bake on the center oven rack for 40 to 45 minutes or until a knife inserted in the center comes out clean. Remove the cake from the oven and cool completely in the pan before serving. Frost if desired.

Store in a sealed container in the refrigerator for up to 1 week or freeze for up to 1 month.

Chocolate Fudge Cake

A rich, dense cake covered in a smooth ganache frosting that will have your guests thinking you bought this cake at a fine bakery. The better the quality of bittersweet or semisweet chocolate (not milk chocolate), the tastier the ganache. If you're using chocolate chunks instead of chocolate chips, chop them into smaller pieces to ensure they melt thoroughly. Make this cake one day before you plan to serve it.

1 cup (250 mL) butter

2 cups (500 mL) semisweet chocolate chips

1¼ cups (310 mL) white or cane sugar

1 cup (250 mL) unsweetened cocoa powder

½ cup (125 mL) quinoa flour

5 large eggs

⅓ cup (80 mL) sour cream

¾ cup (185 mL) whipping cream (35%)

1 tsp (5 mL) pure vanilla extract

2 cups (500 mL) fresh raspberries (optional)

Preheat the oven to 350°F (180°C). Lightly grease a 10-inch (25 cm) springform pan or spray with cooking oil. Fit a piece of parchment paper into the bottom of the pan.

Melt the butter in a small saucepan on medium-low heat. Stir in 1 cup (250 mL) of the chocolate chips until almost melted. Remove the saucepan from the heat.

Whisk the sugar, cocoa powder and flour in a large bowl until well combined. Whisk in the eggs and sour cream until thoroughly mixed. Whisk in the chocolate-butter mixture. Pour the batter into the pan and bake on the center oven rack for 40 to 45 minutes or until a knife comes out clean when inserted in the center of the cake. Remove the cake from the oven and place a piece of foil over the top of the cake pan to keep the top of the cake from drying out. Cool the cake.

When the cake is completely cool, remove the outer ring. Invert onto a flat platter and remove the parchment paper.

Place the remaining 1 cup (250 mL) of chocolate chips in a medium bowl. Heat the whipping cream in a small saucepan to boiling (watch it carefully, and don't let it boil over). Pour the hot cream over the chocolate chips and whisk until smooth. Blend in the vanilla. Let cool briefly (3 minutes) and then pour carefully over the cake, starting in the center of the cake and spiraling outward. Continue until the cake is covered. Tip: If you run out of ganache before you reach the outer edge, pick up the platter and slightly tilt it, allowing the ganache to spread. Refrigerate the cake until completely chilled. Garnish with raspberries (if using). Store covered in the refrigerator for up to 1 week.

Blueberry Sponge Cake

This sponge cake is served hot and is wonderful à la mode.

2 cups (500 mL) blueberries, fresh
   or frozen
⅓ cup (80 mL) white or cane sugar
1 large egg
⅓ cup (80 mL) packed brown
   sugar

⅓ cup (80 mL) butter, melted
½ cup (125 mL) milk
1 cup (250 mL) quinoa flour

Preheat the oven to 350°F (180°C). Lightly grease an 8-inch (20 cm) round baking dish or spray with cooking oil.

Combine the blueberries and sugar in a small bowl, mixing until the blueberries are evenly coated. Spoon the mixture evenly into the bottom of the baking dish.

Whisk the egg and brown sugar in a medium bowl. Add the butter and milk and stir until well blended. Fold in the flour and gently mix until smooth. Pour the batter into the baking dish over the blueberries.

Bake on the center oven rack for 25 to 30 minutes, until the top is golden brown. Slice and serve hot, carefully lifting out the cake and spooning the blueberry sauce on top.

Serves 9.

Caramel Date Cake

Our version of the popular "sticky toffee pudding," this luxurious cake is deliciously moist and best served the same day it is baked. Great topped with whipped cream or ice cream.

Cake	
1¾ cups (435 mL) chopped pitted dates	1 tsp (5 mL) baking soda
1 cup (250 mL) boiling water	½ cup (125 mL) butter, softened
1 cup (250 mL) all-purpose flour	1 cup (250 mL) packed brown sugar
¾ cup (185 mL) quinoa flour	2 large eggs
2 tsp (10 mL) baking powder	½ tsp (2 mL) pure vanilla extract

Topping	
¾ cup (185 mL) cream (18%)	⅓ cup (80 mL) butter
1 cup (250 mL) packed brown sugar	½ cup (125 mL) chopped pecans

Preheat the oven to 350°F (180°C). Grease a 9-inch (23 cm) square baking pan or spray with cooking oil.

In a medium bowl, combine the dates and boiling water and set aside so the dates absorb the water.

In a separate, large bowl, combine the all-purpose and quinoa flours, baking powder and baking soda. Blend well.

Place the butter, brown sugar, eggs and vanilla in a large bowl and beat well. Add the flour mixture and continue to mix until well blended. Fold in the dates. Pour the batter into the pan.

Bake on the center oven rack for 35 minutes.

Combine the cream, sugar and butter in a medium saucepan over high heat and bring to a boil. Reduce the heat to medium-low and stir constantly until the mixture is a thick caramel sauce, about 15 to 20 minutes.

Remove the cake from the oven and pour three-quarters of the caramel sauce on top. Return the cake to the oven for an additional 5 minutes. Remove from the oven and allow to cool slightly. Sprinkle with chopped pecans. Cut into 9 pieces and serve warm. Drizzle individual slices with the remaining caramel sauce.

Lemon Poppy Seed Loaf

Fresh, tart lemons bring this loaf to life. Don't settle for artificial flavors. This loaf won't last long.

1 cup (250 mL) sugar
½ cup (125 mL) butter, softened
3 large eggs
½ cup (125 mL) light sour cream
1 tsp (5 mL) pure vanilla extract
1½ cups (375 mL) quinoa flour

2 tsp (10 mL) baking powder
¼ tsp (1 mL) salt
3 Tbsp (45 mL) poppy seeds
2 Tbsp (30 mL) grated lemon zest
  (about 2 lemons)

Glaze ⅓ cup (80 mL) fresh lemon juice
    (about 1–2 lemons)

½ cup (125 mL) sugar

Preheat the oven to 350°F (180°C). Lightly grease an 8- × 4-inch (1.5 L) loaf pan, spray with cooking oil or line the bottom with parchment paper.

Cream the sugar and butter in a large bowl. Add the eggs, sour cream and vanilla. Whisk together until the mixture has a smooth and creamy consistency.

Combine the flour, baking powder, salt, poppy seeds and lemon zest in a medium bowl. Mix well.

Add the flour mixture to the butter and egg mixture and whisk until smooth. Pour the batter into the loaf pan and bake on the center oven rack for 40 to 45 minutes, until a toothpick inserted in the center comes out clean. Remove and cool completely in the pan.

Combine the lemon juice and sugar in a small saucepan over medium heat. Stir constantly until the sugar has completely dissolved. Set aside to cool.

When the loaf has cooled, remove it from the pan. Holding the loaf carefully, poke small holes with a toothpick all over the sides and bottom. Brush half the lemon glaze over the sides and bottom. Lastly, poke holes in the top of the loaf and brush with the remaining glaze. Slice and serve. Store in a sealed container in the refrigerator for up to 1 week.

Cranberry Orange Loaf

This loaf has the perfect amount of sweetness, allowing the flavors of cranberry and orange to shine through. To make this gluten-free, use tapioca flour instead of all-purpose flour.

⅔ cup (160 mL) white or golden quinoa

1⅓ cups (330 mL) water

½ cup (125 mL) orange juice

¼ cup (60 mL) vegetable oil

2 large eggs

1 Tbsp (15 mL) grated orange zest

1 tsp (5 mL) pure vanilla extract

½ cup (125 mL) all-purpose flour or tapioca flour

⅓ cup (80 mL) white or cane sugar

2 tsp (10 mL) baking powder

¼ tsp (1 mL) salt

1 cup (250 mL) dried cranberries

Bring the water and quinoa to a boil in a medium saucepan. Cover, reduce to a simmer and cook for 10 minutes. Turn the heat off and leave on the burner, covered, for another 10 minutes. Fluff with a fork and allow the quinoa to cool.

Preheat the oven to 350°F (180°C). Lightly grease a 9- × 5-inch (2 L) loaf pan or spray with cooking oil. Cut a piece of parchment paper to fit the bottom for easy removal of the loaf after baking.

Combine the orange juice, oil, eggs, orange zest and vanilla in a blender or food processor. Add 2 cups (500 mL) of the cooked quinoa and purée the mixture until fairly smooth.

Mix the flour, sugar, baking powder and salt in a large bowl. Add the cranberries and stir until completely coated in the flour mixture. Mix in the quinoa-orange purée. Pour the mixture into the loaf pan. Bake on the center oven rack for 45 to 55 minutes, until a knife inserted in the center comes out clean. Allow the loaf to cool in the pan. Remove from the pan, slice and serve. Store in a sealed container in the refrigerator for up to 4 days or freeze for up to 1 month.

Serves 6–8.

Pineapple Upside-Down Loaf

The pineapple is often regarded as a symbol of hospitality. Sliced and served with a small crown of whipped cream, this sweet dessert will definitely charm your guests.

⅓ cup (80 mL) butter	⅓ cup (80 mL) white sugar
⅔ cup (160 mL) packed brown sugar	2 tsp (10 mL) baking powder
	¼ tsp (1 mL) salt
One 19 oz (540 mL) can pineapple chunks, drained	⅓ cup (80 mL) butter, softened
	⅔ cup (160 mL) buttermilk
⅔ cup (160 mL) all-purpose flour	1 large egg
⅔ cup (160 mL) quinoa flour	½ tsp (2 mL) pure vanilla extract

Preheat the oven to 350°F (180°C). Lightly grease an 8- × 4-inch (1.5 L) loaf pan or spray with cooking oil.

Combine the butter and brown sugar in a small saucepan over medium heat and cook until the sugar dissolves. Add the pineapple chunks. Pour half of this mixture into the bottom of the loaf pan and set the remainder aside.

In a medium bowl, combine the all-purpose flour, quinoa flour, white sugar, baking powder and salt. In a separate bowl, blend the butter, buttermilk, egg and vanilla. Add the butter and egg mixture to the flour mixture and blend well. Spoon the batter into the loaf pan, on top of the pineapple. Add the remainder of the pineapple mixture to the top of the batter mixture. Using a knife, gently swirl the pineapple mixture into the surface of the batter.

Bake on the center oven rack for 45 minutes or until a toothpick inserted in the center comes out clean. Remove from the oven. Allow the loaf to cool for at least 20 minutes in the pan before flipping upside down onto a plate. Slice and serve.

Pumpkin Loaf

This deliciously moist pumpkin loaf will fill your kitchen with the comforting smell of autumn spices. Make it extra luxurious by topping it with the cream cheese frosting recipe from the Carrot Cake (page 157). (You will only need to make half the frosting.)

2¼ cups (560 mL) quinoa flour
1 cup (250 mL) all-purpose flour
2 tsp (10 mL) baking soda
1 tsp (5 mL) ground cinnamon
1 tsp (5 mL) ground nutmeg
½ tsp (2 mL) salt
⅔ cup (160 mL) milk
1 Tbsp (15 mL) white vinegar
2 cups (500 mL) pumpkin purée
¾ cup (185 mL) packed brown sugar
¾ cup (185 mL) white sugar
½ cup (125 mL) applesauce
½ cup (125 mL) vegetable oil
4 large eggs

Preheat the oven to 350°F (180°C). Lightly grease two 9- × 5-inch (2 L) loaf pans or spray with cooking oil.

In a large bowl, combine the quinoa flour, all-purpose flour, baking soda, cinnamon, nutmeg and salt.

Combine the milk and vinegar in a small bowl and set aside. In a separate, large bowl, blend the pumpkin, brown sugar, white sugar, applesauce and vegetable oil together. Add the sour milk and eggs and blend well.

Distribute the batter equally between the pans. Bake for 55 to 60 minutes on the center oven rack. Remove from the oven and cool completely in the pan before slicing and serving.

Raspberry Cake

This raspberry cake is light and airy, a perfect luxury for a summer afternoon tea.

½ cup (125 mL) butter, softened
¾ cup (185 mL) white sugar
1 cup (250 mL) sour cream
2 large eggs
1 tsp (5 mL) pure vanilla extract
1 cup (250 mL) quinoa flour
1 cup (250 mL) all-purpose flour
1½ tsp (7.5 mL) baking powder
1½ tsp (7.5 mL) baking soda
2 cups (500 mL) fresh (or frozen) raspberries
½ cup (125 mL) packed brown sugar
1 tsp (5 mL) ground cinnamon
2 Tbsp (30 mL) butter, melted

Preheat the oven to 375°F (190°C). Lightly grease a 9-inch (23 cm) square baking pan or spray with cooking oil and line with parchment paper.

Combine the softened butter and white sugar in a large bowl. Add the sour cream, eggs and vanilla and mix thoroughly. In a separate bowl, combine the quinoa and all-purpose flours, baking powder and baking soda. Gently toss the raspberries with the flour mixture. Add the flour mixture to the butter mixture and blend well.

Pour the batter into the baking pan and set aside. Combine the brown sugar, cinnamon and melted butter and drizzle over the cake.

Bake on the center oven rack for 40 to 45 minutes. Remove from the oven and cool completely before cutting into squares and serving.

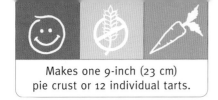

Makes one 9-inch (23 cm)
pie crust or 12 individual tarts.

Makes one 9-inch (23 cm)
tart crust or 12 individual tarts.

Basic Pie Crust

The combination of flours makes a stable, no-roll crust suitable for liquid fillings such as fruit. It has a less nutty flavor than the Basic Tart Crust (recipe at right) and is slightly less flaky than a regular flour pie crust. Leave out the cinnamon and sugar if the crust is required for a savory dish such as a quiche. To make this gluten-free, use tapioca flour in place of the whole wheat flour.

1 cup (250 mL) quinoa flour
¼ cup (60 mL) whole wheat flour or tapioca flour
3 Tbsp (45 mL) white or cane sugar (optional)
½ tsp (2 mL) ground cinnamon (optional)
½ cup (125 mL) butter, melted and slightly cooled
1 Tbsp (15 mL) water

Preheat the oven to 350°F (180°C). Combine the quinoa and whole wheat flours, and sugar and cinnamon if using, in a medium bowl and mix well. Blend in the melted butter. Add the water and use your hands to form a soft dough. Press evenly into a lightly greased 9-inch (23 cm) pie plate.

If baking the shell empty, bake on the center oven rack for 10 to 12 minutes. Allow to cool completely before adding a filling.

If baking filled, bake according to the original recipe instructions, covering with foil if the edges become dark. Note: If using a liquid filling such as fruit, prebake the crust for 7 to 8 minutes prior to filling and baking.

Basic Tart Crust

This healthier pastry alternative will work with most of your favorite fillings. This tart crust has a slightly nutty flavor that works well for cheesecakes, tarts or even quiches. Leave out the sugar if making it for a savory dish such as quiche.

1¼ cups (310 mL) quinoa flour
3 Tbsp (45 mL) white or cane sugar
½ cup (125 mL) butter, softened
1 Tbsp (15 mL) water

Combine the flour and sugar in a large bowl. Cut in the butter and use your fingers to make a soft crumble. Drizzle in the water and use your hands to form a soft dough. Refrigerate for 45 to 60 minutes.

Preheat the oven to 375°F (190°C). Grease a 9-inch (23 cm) pie plate or spray with cooking oil to make it easier to remove from the pie plate. On a lightly floured surface, roll the dough into a circle large enough to fit inside the pie plate. You may have to pull and press the dough to fit the entire pie plate.

If baking the shell empty, poke a few holes in the bottom with a fork to ensure the tart crust bakes flat. Bake on the center oven rack for 15 minutes. Remove from the oven. Allow to completely cool before adding the filling.

If baking filled, bake according to the original recipe instructions, covering with foil if the edges become dark.

Serves 8.

Caramel Pecan Pumpkin Pie

Impress your guests with this dressed-up pumpkin pie topped with caramelized pecans. To make this gluten-free, use tapioca flour instead of whole wheat flour.

One recipe Basic Pie Crust (page 169), unbaked

Filling

One 14 oz (398 mL) can pumpkin purée (or ¾ cup/185 mL fresh pumpkin purée)
2 large eggs
½ cup (125 mL) milk
½ cup (125 mL) packed brown sugar

2 Tbsp (30 mL) quinoa flour
½ tsp (2 mL) salt
½ tsp (2 mL) ground cinnamon
½ tsp (2 mL) ground mace
¼ tsp (1 mL) ground nutmeg
¼ tsp (1 mL) ground ginger

Topping

1 cup (250 mL) pecan pieces
⅓ cup (80 mL) packed brown sugar

2 Tbsp (30 mL) butter, melted
1 cup (250 mL) whipping cream (35%) (optional)

Preheat the oven to 350°F (180°C). Prepare the pie crust. Do not bake. Set aside.

Whisk the pumpkin, eggs, milk and sugar in a medium bowl. Add the flour, salt, cinnamon, mace, nutmeg and ginger and whisk to combine. Pour into the pie crust. Bake for 25 minutes on the center oven rack.

Combine the pecans, sugar and melted butter in a small bowl, mixing until the pecans are lightly coated with sugar. Briefly remove the pie from the oven and sprinkle the pecan mixture evenly overtop. Reduce the oven temperature to 350°F (180°C). Return the pie to the oven and bake for an additional 20 to 25 minutes or until the filling is firm in the center. If the pie appears to be getting too dark, place a piece of foil loosely over the pie and continue baking for the remaining time. Remove from the oven and cool completely. Whip the cream (if using) and serve alongside the pie.

Very Berry Pie *with* Crumble Crust

Quinoa flour makes a fabulous crust with a nutty, toasted flavor that goes beauti-fully with baked berries. It's especially nice served à la mode. To make this recipe gluten-free, use tapioca flour instead of all-purpose flour in the pie crust.

One recipe Basic Pie Crust (page 169), unbaked

Filling

4 cups (1 L) frozen blueberries or mixed berries

⅓ cup (80 mL) white or cane sugar

¼ cup (60 mL) cornstarch

1 Tbsp (15 mL) fresh lemon juice

1 tsp (5 mL) grated lemon zest

Topping

⅓ cup (80 mL) packed brown sugar

¾ cup (185 mL) rolled oats (either quick-cooking or large-flake)

¼ cup (60 mL) quinoa flour

½ tsp (2 mL) ground cinnamon

¼ cup (60 mL) butter, melted

Preheat the oven to 350°F (180°C). (If using a metal pie plate, bake at 325°F/160°C).

Prepare the pie crust. Bake for 8 minutes, remove from the oven and set aside.

Toss the frozen berries, sugar, cornstarch, lemon juice and lemon zest in a large bowl. Spread the fruit over the crust and set aside.

Combine the brown sugar, oats, quinoa flour and cinnamon in a small bowl. Work in the melted butter until well combined. Sprinkle evenly over the fruit.

Bake on the center oven rack for 30 minutes. Remove the pan from the oven and cover with foil to prevent the pie from browning too much. Return the pie to the oven and bake for another 25 to 30 minutes, until the fruit is bubbling at the edges. Remove the pie from the oven and allow to cool completely. Serve with vanilla ice cream if desired.

Caramelized Banana Pudding

The bananas are caramelized in a pan and blended with quinoa and cream for an aromatic delight that is easy to make and easy to eat.

⅔ cup (160 mL) water

⅓ cup (80 mL) quinoa

2 Tbsp (30 mL) butter

¼ cup (60 mL) packed brown sugar

1¼ cups (310 mL) sliced fresh bananas

1 cup (250 mL) whipping cream (35%)

Bring the water and quinoa to a boil in a medium saucepan. Cover, reduce to a simmer and cook for 10 minutes. Turn the heat off and leave the covered saucepan on the burner for another 15 minutes. Fluff with a fork and allow the quinoa to cool.

Melt the butter in a medium saucepan over medium heat. Stir in the sugar and add the bananas. Cook until the bananas are warm and completely coated with the sugar-butter mixture. Remove the saucepan from the heat. Stir in the quinoa.

Whip the cream and fold it into the banana-quinoa mixture. Serve immediately.

Creamy Quinoa Pudding

This is the quinoa version of tapioca pudding. It is nutritionally enhanced and takes less time to make, but it's just as delicious. Try something different by topping the pudding with fresh berries or substituting your favorite liqueur for the vanilla.

⅓ cup (80 mL) quinoa	2 large eggs
⅔ cup (160 mL) water	¼ cup (60 mL) white or cane sugar
2 cups (500 mL) half and half	2 Tbsp (30 mL) cornstarch
cream (10–12%)	½ tsp (2 mL) pure vanilla extract

Bring the quinoa and water to a boil in a medium saucepan. Cover, reduce to a simmer and cook for 10 minutes. Turn the heat off and leave the covered saucepan on the burner for another 6 minutes. Fluff with a fork and allow the quinoa to cool.

Place the cream in a medium saucepan and heat on medium-high until hot but not boiling (steam will rise from the top). Remove from the heat.

Whisk the eggs, sugar and cornstarch with 1 Tbsp (15 mL) of the hot cream in a small bowl. Add an additional 3 Tbsp (45 mL) of hot cream, 1 Tbsp (15 mL) at a time, whisking constantly. Whisk the tempered egg mixture into the saucepan and return to medium heat. Cook, whisking constantly, until the pudding has thickened. Remove from the heat and stir in the quinoa and vanilla. Pour the pudding into individual serving bowls. Cover and chill in the refrigerator until serving time.

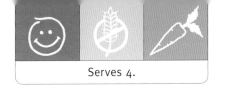

Serves 4.

Decadent Chocolate Pudding

Decadence in an instant! A quick, rich chocolate dessert, full of protein, that's sure to impress your guests.

½ cup (125 mL) quinoa flour
1½ cups (375 mL) water
1 cup (250 mL) semisweet
   chocolate chips
1 cup (250 mL) ricotta cheese

¾ cup (185 mL) whipping
   cream (35%)
1 Tbsp (15 mL) icing sugar
Fresh raspberries or strawberries
   (optional)

Combine the flour and water in a medium saucepan on medium heat. Stir constantly until the mixture is thickened and the water has been absorbed, 3 to 5 minutes. Don't worry if lumps form; these will disappear later. Remove from the heat, immediately add the chocolate chips and stir until melted. Stir in the ricotta cheese. Use a food processor or blender to purée the mixture until smooth and evenly blended. Pour into dessert bowls and refrigerate until chilled.

Just before serving, whip the cream and icing sugar with a whisk or electric mixer until stiff peaks form. Top each serving with whipped cream. Garnish with fresh berries (if using). Serve immediately.

Serves 2.

Peanut Butter *and* Banana Pudding

There is no age limit for enjoying this recipe and it can be eaten anytime—there is simply nothing unhealthy about it. If you have leftover cooked quinoa in the refrigerator, add ⅓ cup (80 mL) instead of the quinoa flour and water. If desired, garnish with slices of fresh banana.

2 Tbsp (30 mL) quinoa flour
¼ cup (60 mL) boiling water
1 frozen banana

½ cup (125 mL) vanilla yogurt
4 tsp (20 mL) peanut butter

Combine the quinoa flour and boiling water in a small bowl and blend together to make a paste. Place the paste in a blender or food processor. Break the frozen banana into chunks and add to the blender. Add the yogurt and peanut butter. Purée until smooth and divide between 2 small bowls. Serve immediately.

Serves 4.

Baked Apples *with* Berries

A nutritious recipe you can feel good about, this is healthy enough to serve as break-fast. To prepare these apples as a dessert, make them a touch sweeter by using an additional 2 Tbsp (30 mL) of brown sugar. The apples can be prepared up to one day in advance, covered and stored in the refrigerator, ready to be baked.

⅔ cup (160 mL) water
⅓ cup (80 mL) quinoa
4 apples, washed and cored (Gala, Golden Delicious or Fiji)
¼ cup (60 mL) sliced almonds
2 Tbsp (30 mL) brown sugar
1 Tbsp (15 mL) fresh lemon juice

1 tsp (5 mL) ground cinnamon
½ tsp (2 mL) ground allspice
1 cup (250 mL) blueberries (thaw if frozen)
1 cup (250 mL) vanilla yogurt or ice cream (optional)

Bring the water and quinoa to a boil in a medium saucepan. Cover, reduce to a simmer and cook for 10 minutes. Turn the heat off and leave the covered saucepan on the burner for another 15 minutes. Fluff with a fork and allow the quinoa to cool.

Preheat the oven to 375°F (190°C). Cut a piece of parchment paper to fit the bottom of a 9-inch (23 cm) square baking dish.

Make a shallow cut around the midsection of each apple (to allow movement of skin during baking). Stand the apples in the baking dish.

Spread the almonds evenly on a baking sheet and bake on the center oven rack for 5 to 7 minutes, until the almonds are fragrant and lightly toasted. Remove from the oven and set aside.

Combine the quinoa and toasted almonds with the sugar, lemon juice, cinnamon and allspice. Add the berries and carefully spoon the quinoa mixture into the cored apples. Spoon the remainder of the quinoa mixture in the pan around the base of the apples. Loosely place a piece of foil over the top of the pan to prevent the apples from burning.

Bake on the center oven rack for 35 to 40 minutes, until the apples are tender. Remove them from the oven and place in individual serving bowls or on dessert plates. Place the additional filling around each apple and top with yogurt or ice cream (if using). Serve immediately.

Note These apples can also be prepared in the microwave for a last-minute dessert. Cook in individual bowls on high for 4 to 5 minutes.

Cran-Apple Crisp

A superb dessert in no time at all! Tart cranberries balance the sweetness of apples, giving the average apple crisp an added dimension.

Fruit	
6 apples, peeled, cored and sliced into ½-inch (1 cm) pieces	¼ cup (60 mL) white or cane sugar
1 cup (250 mL) cranberries, fresh or frozen	1 tsp (5 mL) ground cinnamon
	2 Tbsp (30 mL) maple syrup (optional)

Topping	
1 cup (250 mL) quinoa flour	½ cup (125 mL) butter
⅓ cup (80 mL) white or cane sugar	1 cup (250 mL) coarsely chopped walnuts, almonds or pecans
¼ cup (60 mL) packed brown sugar	Vanilla ice cream (optional)

Preheat the oven to 350°F (180°C). Grease a 9- × 13-inch (3.5 L) baking dish or spray with cooking oil.

Combine the apples and cranberries in a medium bowl. Add the sugar and cinnamon and toss to evenly coat the fruit. Stir in the maple syrup (if using). Pour the mixture into the baking dish.

Combine the flour, both sugars and butter in a medium bowl. Using your hands, blend until the mixture has a crumbly consistency. Stir in the nuts and spoon evenly over the apple mixture. Place in the oven and bake on the center rack for 45 to 50 minutes, until the fruit is bubbling through the topping. Serve warm and top with ice cream (if using).

Serves 4–6.

Strawberry Rhubarb Crumble

Rhubarb and strawberry mingle perfectly with the nutty flavor of quinoa, oats and cinnamon. This crumble is best with vanilla ice cream.

3 cups (750 mL) strawberries, quartered

2 cups (500 mL) chopped rhubarb (½-inch/1 cm pieces)

½ cup (125 mL) white or cane sugar

3 Tbsp (45 mL) cornstarch

2 tsp (10 mL) ground cinnamon

¾ cup (185 mL) quick-cooking rolled oats

½ cup (125 mL) firmly packed brown sugar

¼ cup (60 mL) quinoa flour

¼ cup (60 mL) melted butter

¼ cup (60 mL) sliced almonds

Preheat the oven to 350°F (180°C) and lightly grease a 9-x 13-inch (3.5 L) baking dish or spray with cooking oil.

Combine the strawberries, rhubarb, white sugar, cornstarch and 1 tsp (5 mL) of the cinnamon in a large bowl. Toss until the ingredients are well combined and spread the mixture in the baking dish.

Combine the oats, brown sugar, flour and the remaining 1 tsp (5 mL) of cinnamon in a medium bowl. Add the melted butter and mix well to form a crumbly mixture. Sprinkle evenly over the fruit and cover the dish with foil. Bake on the center oven rack for 30 minutes. Remove the foil and sprinkle with the sliced almonds. Return to the oven for another 25 minutes or until the fruit is bubbling and the rhubarb is tender. Remove the crisp from the oven and let rest 8 to 10 minutes before serving.

Fresh Fruit Quinoa Parfaits

A scrumptious, fluffy and creamy dessert that is completely guilt-free. Perfect in fresh berry season and delicious year-round with frozen berries. Try sliced fresh peaches, mango, kiwi, papaya, pineapple, strawberries, blueberries, raspberries, blackberries, applesauce or bananas. For an even fruitier flavor, substitute any of your favorite fruit yogurts for the plain yogurt, vanilla extract and maple syrup.

½ cup (125 mL) water
¼ cup (60 mL) quinoa
1 cup (250 mL) plain yogurt
1 tsp (5 mL) maple syrup or brown
   sugar

¼ tsp (1 mL) pure vanilla extract
¾ cup (185 mL) fresh berries or
   diced fresh or frozen fruit of
   your choice
Fresh mint (optional)

Bring the water and quinoa to a boil in a small saucepan. Reduce to a simmer, cover and cook for 10 minutes. Turn the heat off but keep the covered saucepan on the burner for an additional 5 minutes. Fluff with a fork and set aside to cool.

In a small bowl, combine the yogurt with the maple syrup and vanilla. Add the quinoa and mix until well blended.

Divide the fruit and yogurt mixture evenly between two 1½-cup (375 mL) parfait glasses (or tall glasses), creating alternate layers of fruit and yogurt. Garnish the top with a single berry and a sprig of fresh mint (if using). Enjoy immediately or refrigerate for up to 2 days.

Chapter 7

EVERYDAY BABY FOOD WITH QUINOA

Nutritious Beginnings

Making your own baby food not only allows you to control all the ingredients your child is eating; it can also be economical compared to buying expensive premade baby foods. The recipes here are arranged roughly in age groupings, but consult your pediatrician when introducing solids, as generalities may not apply to your baby. When using multiple ingredients as you would in toddler food, ensure your child safely enjoys each of the ingredients individually prior to introducing combinations.

Puréed combinations of quinoa, fruit and vegetables make tasty and nutritious baby food. We find it's best to use organic ingredients wherever possible. It may cost a bit more, but organic foods are higher in quality and often better tasting. Create your own baby food recipes, using quinoa puréed, strained (if necessary) and thinned with milk or water to make a great cereal or cereal base.

The quinoa in these recipes is virtually undetectable and enhances the food's texture, making it smooth and creamy. Convenient and practical, some of these recipes can be frozen in individual portions and stored in resealable freezer bags for up to 2 months. To serve frozen portions, thaw them in the refrigerator or warm slowly over low heat in a small saucepan. Once thawed, baby food can be refrigerated for up to 48 hours.

QUINOA SEEDS, FLAKES AND FLOUR

Whole **quinoa seeds** (as compared to quinoa flakes or flour) make optimal baby food because nutrition is best maintained in a whole grain. We recommend using white or golden quinoa for baby food because the seeds tend to cook softer and are better for making a smooth purée. Ensure it is puréed well and press it through a strainer if you need a finer consistency.

In 30 minutes or less, you can prepare your own baby food blends with cooked quinoa. Simply place the quinoa and water in an appropriate saucepan and bring to a boil. Cover, reduce to a simmer and cook for 10 minutes. Turn the heat off and keep the covered saucepan on the burner for another 20 to 25 minutes to ensure the quinoa is well cooked, fluffy and soft. Allow the quinoa to cool before processing.

RATIOS FOR QUINOA SEEDS

1 cup (250 mL) uncooked quinoa, 2½ cups (625 mL) water =
    4 cups (1 L) cooked
½ cup (125 mL) uncooked quinoa, 1¼ cups (310 mL) water =
    2 cups (500 mL) cooked
¼ cup (60 mL) uncooked quinoa, ⅔ cup (160 mL) water =
    1 cup (250 mL) cooked

Quinoa flakes are a quick option that can be used for any meal as an alternative to oatmeal. They have a mild flavor and take about 4 minutes to prepare. For almost instant baby food, combine quinoa flakes and water in an appropriate saucepan and bring to a boil, uncovered. Reduce the heat and cook at a simmer for 3 to 4 minutes, stirring occasionally, until the flakes are soft and extremely tender. Remove the saucepan from the heat. Dilute with water, juice or whatever milk you are nourishing your baby with to give the flakes the desired consistency and flavor.

1 cup (250 mL) quinoa flakes, 2⅔ cups (660 mL) water =
   2⅔ cups (660 mL) cooked

½ cup (125 mL) quinoa flakes, 1½ cups (375 mL) water =
   1½ cups (375 mL) cooked

¼ cup (60 mL) quinoa flakes, ⅔ cup (160 mL) water =
   ⅔ cup (160 mL) cooked

Another "instant" option for preparing nutrition-packed quinoa baby food is **quinoa flour**. Quinoa flour is a bit more expensive and has a stronger fragrance and taste than all-purpose flour, so begin incorporating it into baby food in small quantities. Buy the best quality you can find on the market, as this will ensure the quinoa has been washed thoroughly and any bitter flavor has been removed.

Place the quinoa flour in a glass or stainless steel bowl and add boiling water according to the ratios below. Stir the mixture together, mashing any lumps with the back of a spoon. Cover with foil and set aside briefly (3 to 5 minutes). Thin with additional milk or water to the desired consistency.

RATIOS FOR QUINOA FLOUR

½ cup (125 mL) quinoa flour, 1½ cups (375 mL) boiling water =
   1½ cups (375 mL) cooked

¼ cup (60 mL) quinoa flour, ¾ cup (185 mL) boiling water =
   ¾ cup (185 mL) cooked

2 Tbsp (30 mL) quinoa flour, ⅓ cup (80 mL) boiling water =
   ⅓ cup (80 mL) cooked

Blueberry Banana Mash

A quick and tasty combination your baby or toddler will enjoy. Freeze for a maximum of two months to maintain the best nutritional value.

⅔ cup (160 mL) ripe banana
⅔ cup (160 mL) fresh or frozen blueberries
⅔ cup (160 mL) cooked quinoa, cooked quinoa
   flakes or quinoa flour
2 Tbsp (30 mL) water or milk (if required)

Blend the banana, blueberries and cooked quinoa together in a food processor or blender. Purée the ingredients until smooth. Thin with water or milk to obtain the desired consistency, or press through a strainer if you require a finer consistency.

Pour the Blueberry Banana Mash into an ice cube tray and freeze for about 5 hours. Remove the cubes and place them in a resealable freezer bag in the freezer for up to 2 months. To serve, simply thaw in the refrigerator. Thawed purée will stay fresh in a sealed container in the refrigerator for up to 48 hours.

Healthy Quinoa Vegetable Purée

Take your pick of vegetables—carrot, sweet potato, broccoli, peas, butternut squash or potato. After your child has been able to eat them separately with success, you can create any combination. Freeze for a maximum of two months for best nutritional value.

1 cup (250 mL) washed, peeled and diced raw
   vegetables
1 cup (250 mL) cooked quinoa, cooked quinoa
   flakes or quinoa flour
¼–⅓ cup (60–80 mL) water, reserved cooking
   liquid or milk

Gently steam the vegetables or simmer in a saucepan with just enough water to cover for about 15 to 20 minutes or until the vegetables are soft. Remove from the heat and allow to cool. Place the vegetables and cooked quinoa in a blender or food processor and purée until smooth. Thin with water, cooking liquid or milk to the desired consistency. Strain the vegetables if a smoother consistency is required.

Pour the purée into an ice cube tray and freeze for about 5 hours. Remove the frozen cubes from the tray and place in a resealable freezer bag in the freezer. To serve, thaw the cubes in the refrigerator or slowly in a small saucepan on the lowest heat. Thawed purée will stay fresh in a sealed container in the refrigerator for up to 48 hours.

Super Quinoa Fruit Purée

Quinoa blended with your choice of fruit, such as apple, pear, peach, blueberries, apricot or plum, is a simple combination for your growing baby's enjoyment and health. Use sweet, ripe fruit for the best nutrition and flavor. After your child has been able to eat each fruit separately with success, you can create any combination.

1 cup (250 mL) washed, pitted, peeled and diced fruit
½ cup (125 mL) water
1 cup (250 mL) cooked quinoa, cooked quinoa flakes or quinoa flour

Combine the diced fruit and water in a large saucepan and bring to a boil. Cover, reduce to a simmer and cook until soft, about 8 to 10 minutes. Remove from the heat and allow to cool.

Place the fruit and cooked quinoa in a blender or food processor. Purée until smooth. Thin the mixture with water, cooking liquid or milk until desired consistency is reached. Strain the fruit if a smoother consistency is required.

Pour the purée into an ice cube tray and freeze for about 5 hours. Remove the frozen cubes from the tray and place in a resealable freezer bag. Freeze for a maximum of 2 months to maintain the best nutritional value. To serve, thaw the cubes either in the refrigerator or in a small saucepan on the lowest setting. Thawed purée will stay fresh in a sealed container in the refrigerator for up to 48 hours.

Chicken Veggie Mélange

This blend of chicken, vegetables and quinoa is a healthy, balanced combination that your child will enjoy. If you need more on hand, this recipe can easily be doubled.

1 cup (250 mL) low-sodium chicken stock or water
½ cup (125 mL) diced cooked chicken breast
½ cup (125 mL) diced raw potato or sweet potato
½ cup (125 mL) diced raw carrots, peas or broccoli
2 Tbsp (30 mL) quinoa, uncooked

Combine the stock, chicken, potato, carrots and quinoa in a small saucepan and bring to a boil. Cover, reduce to a simmer and cook for about 25 to 30 minutes, until the vegetables are soft. Remove from the heat and allow the mixture to cool.

Purée in a food processor or blender. Thin the mixture with water to reach the desired consistency. Pour the purée into an ice cube tray and freeze for about 5 hours. Remove the frozen cubes from the tray and place into a resealable freezer bag. Freeze for a maximum of 2 months to maintain the best nutritional value. To serve, thaw in the refrigerator or in a saucepan on the lowest setting. Thawed purée will stay fresh in a sealed container in the refrigerator for up to 48 hours.

Chicken, Quinoa *and* Apple Purée

Chicken and apples are an enjoyable combination for babies, especially if they are fussy with a plain chicken purée.

⅔ cup (160 mL) applesauce or cooked apples

¼ cup (60 mL) diced cooked chicken breast

¼ cup (60 mL) cooked quinoa, cooked quinoa flakes or quinoa flour

Combine the applesauce, chicken and quinoa in a blender or food processor. Purée until smooth. Thin with water, chicken stock or milk until the desired consistency is reached. Pour into an ice cube tray and freeze for about 5 hours. Remove the frozen cubes and place them into a resealable freezer bag. Freeze for a maximum of 2 months to maintain the best nutritional value. To serve, thaw the cubes in the refrigerator or in a saucepan on the lowest setting. Thawed purée will stay fresh in a sealed container for up to 48 hours in the refrigerator.

Fine Fruit Smoothie

A fast smoothie your child can enjoy any time of the day. For a cool snack on those hot days, try using frozen fruit and plain frozen yogurt. Double the recipe so you can enjoy some, too!

½ cup (125 mL) plain yogurt

2 Tbsp (30 mL) cooked quinoa, cooked quinoa flakes or quinoa flour

2 Tbsp (30 mL) fruit (strawberries, blueberries, banana, mango)

2 Tbsp (30 mL) milk

1 tsp (5 mL) maple syrup

Combine the yogurt, quinoa, fruit, milk and syrup in a blender or food processor. Purée until completely smooth. Serve immediately.

Quinoa Cheese Fruit Cup

Use fruit that is in season to create this quick, satisfying lunch or snack.

¼ cup (60 mL) cottage cheese (2%)

2 Tbsp (30 mL) cooked quinoa, cooked quinoa flakes or quinoa flour

2 Tbsp (30 mL) peeled, finely chopped fruit (kiwi, banana, papaya, mango, strawberries, blueberries, peach, plum or pear)

Combine the cottage cheese and quinoa in a small bowl. Stir the chopped fruit on top. Best if enjoyed immediately.

Banana Chocolate Chip Babycakes

These mini pancakes are great for breakfast or a snack. Use blueberries in place of chocolate chips for an even healthier option. Freeze these little handheld gems for convenient snacks and emergency meals.

1⅓ cups (330 mL) quinoa flour

3 Tbsp (45 mL) white or cane sugar

1 Tbsp (15 mL) baking powder

½ tsp (2 mL) salt

1¼ cups (310 mL) milk

1 large egg

1 Tbsp (15 mL) vegetable oil

1 tsp (5 mL) pure vanilla extract

1 cup (250 mL) mashed ripe
    banana

⅓ cup (80 mL) chocolate chips or
    blueberries

Combine the flour, sugar, baking powder and salt in a large bowl.

Whisk the milk, egg, vegetable oil and vanilla in a medium bowl. Whisk in the mashed banana until thoroughly combined. Pour the banana and milk mixture into the flour mixture. Whisk together until well blended.

Lightly grease a large nonstick frying pan or spray with cooking oil and place over medium heat. When the pan is hot, use a tablespoon or soup ladle (depending on the size of pancake you want) to pour batter into the pan. (This recipe makes twenty-six 2-inch/5 cm mini pancakes or thirteen 4-inch/10 cm pancakes.) Add a few chocolate chips or blueberries on top of each pancake. Cook the pancakes until bubbles form around the edges, then flip and cook the other side until lightly browned. Remove the pancakes from the pan and cool slightly before serving (the chocolate or blueberries will be extra hot). Serve with pure maple syrup or yogurt or simply eat them like biscuits. Freeze in resealable freezer bags for up to 1 month.

Chicken, Broccoli *and* Cheese Quinoa

A good dose of veggies and quinoa enhanced with the flavors of chicken and cheese makes for a yummy meal. Switch it up by using peas or cauliflower in place of broccoli.

½ cup (125 mL) cooked broccoli, peas or cauliflower

½ cup (125 mL) water, chicken broth or vegetable cooking water

⅓ cup (80 mL) cooked quinoa, quinoa flakes or quinoa flour

2 Tbsp (30 mL) finely diced cooked chicken breast

2 Tbsp (30 mL) shredded cheddar cheese

Blend all the ingredients together in a food processor or blender until smooth or at a desired consistency for the age of your baby (this recipe freezes best when puréed). Thin with water if necessary and freeze in an ice cube tray for about 5 hours.

Remove the frozen cubes from the tray and store in a resealable freezer bag in the freezer. To serve, thaw the cubes in the refrigerator or in a saucepan on the lowest heat setting. Freeze for a maximum of 2 months to maintain the best nutritional value. Thawed purée will stay fresh for up to 48 hours in a sealed container in the refrigerator.

Natural Strawberry Quinoa Yogurt

A chunkier mixture for the growing toddler, this combination introduces whole quinoa and small fruit pieces together with yogurt and a touch of natural maple syrup sweetness.

¼ cup (60 mL) plain yogurt

2 Tbsp (30 mL) cooked quinoa, quinoa flakes or quinoa flour

2 Tbsp (30 mL) finely diced fresh strawberries (or other fruit)

½ tsp (2 mL) maple syrup

Combine the yogurt, quinoa, strawberries and maple syrup in a small bowl and mix well. Serve fresh. Do not freeze.

INDEX

Page numbers in color indicate recipes with a photo.

Aa

almonds
Cauliflower and Broccoli Bake with Toasted Almonds 42
Chocolate Almond Biscotti 139
Fresh Cucumber and Toasted Almond Salad with Dill 48
Mandarin Almond Salad 49
Pomegranate, Almond and Feta Salad 50

apples
Apple Cinnamon Cheesecake 155
Apple-Glazed Pork Chops on Quinoa 92
Apple Strudel Breakfast Cereal 13
Apple Toffee Cake 156
Baked Apples with Berries 177
Chicken, Quinoa and Apple Purée 187
Cran-Apple Crisp 178
Asian Sprout Salad 45
Asparagus with Lime Cilantro Sauce, Salmon and Red Quinoa on 97

avocado
Chilled Avocado Soup 63
Quinoa Guacam-Óle! 36

Bb

baby food 4, 10, 182–84
freezing 182
recipes 185–91
Baked Potato, The Perfect 122

banana
Banana Chocolate Chip Babycakes 190
Blueberry Banana Mash 185
Caramelized Banana Pudding 173
Chocolate Quinoa Crepes with Bananas 20
Peanut Butter and Banana Pudding 176
Strawberry Banana Muffins 130
bars and squares. See also cookies
Breakfast Fruit and Oatmeal Bars 32
Date Squares 148
Raspberry Coconut Bars 149

Toffee Mocha Squares 145
Basic Pie Crust 169
Basic Tart Crust 169
beans. See also chickpeas
Black Bean Nacho Dip 35
Black Bean Quinoa Quesadillas 41
Black Bean Soup 59
Chili 94
Hearty Beans and Greens Stew 75
Maple Bean Tarts 150
Mexican Casserole 111
Quinoa Bean Dip 35
Quinoa Bean Salad 52
Southwestern Quinoa 110
Southwest Quinoa Salad 54

beef
Beef and Sweet Potato Tagine on Quinoa 77
Beef Vegetable Quinoa Soup 61
Buffalo Quinoa Potage 78
Chili 94
Ginger Edamame Quinoa (optional ingredient) 82
Greek Burgers 117
Peruvian Peppered Steak on Quinoa 93
Santa Fe Meatballs 40
Beet Soup, Dill 65
berries
Baked Apples with Berries 177
Berry Flax Bran Muffins 128
Blueberry Banana Mash 185
Blueberry Flax Hot Cereal 13
Blueberry Flax Pancakes (variation) 24
Blueberry Sponge Cake 162
Blueberry Vanilla Smoothie 30
Cran-Apple Crisp 178
Cranberry Orange Loaf 166
Fine Fruit Smoothie 187
Fresh Fruit Quinoa Parfaits 180
Hot Cranberry Date Cereal 14
Lemon Blueberry Muffins 129
Natural Strawberry Quinoa Yogurt 191
Raspberry Cake 168

Raspberry Coconut Bars 149
Raspberry Cream Cheese Muffins 127
Strawberry Banana Muffins 130
Strawberry Rhubarb Crumble 179
Strawberry Shake 30
Super Fiber Cereal 16
Very Berry Pie with Crumble Crust 172
Biscotti, Chocolate Almond 139
Biscuits, Herb 152
black beans
Black Bean Nacho Dip 35
Black Bean Quinoa Quesadillas 41
Black Bean Soup 59
Chili 94
Mexican Casserole 111
Southwestern Quinoa 110
Southwest Quinoa Salad 54
blueberries
Baked Apples with Berries 177
Berry Flax Bran Muffins 128
Blueberry Banana Mash 185
Blueberry Flax Hot Cereal 13
Blueberry Flax Pancakes (variation) 24
Blueberry Sponge Cake 162
Blueberry Vanilla Smoothie 30
Lemon Blueberry Muffins 129
Very Berry Pie with Crumble Crust 172
Bocconcini and Oregano Salad 47
Bran Muffins, Berry Flax 128
Bran Muffins, Raisin 125
bread. See also loaves
Cheddar Cheese Bread (variation) 151
Irish Soda Bread 151
Outrageously Quick and Easy Pizza Crust 120
Rosemary Parmesan Bread (variation) 151
broccoli
Broccoli Cheese Soup 62
Broccoli Goat Cheese Soufflé 103
Cauliflower and Broccoli Bake with Toasted Almonds 42

Chicken, Broccoli and Cheese Quinoa 191

Chicken Broccoli Casserole 81

Mushroom Broccoli Quisotto 44

Thai Cashew Chicken and Broccoli on Quinoa 88

Vegetable Cheddar Quiche 106

Brownies, Chocolate Cheesecake 146

Brownies, Chocolate Truffle 147

buffalo

Buffalo Quinoa Potage 78

Chili (optional ingredient) 94

burgers

Garden Burger, The 119

Greek Burgers 117

Light Open-Faced Salmon Burgers 118

Burritos, Quinoa Breakfast 27

Cc

cake. *See also* loaves

Apple Cinnamon Cheesecake 155

Apple Toffee Cake 156

Blueberry Sponge Cake 162

Caramel Date Cake 163

Carrot Cake 157

Chocolate Fudge Cake 160

Date Squares 148

Moist Chocolate Cake 159

Raspberry Cake 168

Caramel Date Cake 163

Caramelized Banana Pudding 173

Caramel Pecan Pumpkin Pie 171

carrot

Carrot Cake 157

Carrot Spice Muffins 126

Curried Carrot Soup 64

Quinoa, Carrot and Lentil Stew 76

Cashew Chicken and Broccoli on Quinoa, Thai 88

Cauliflower and Broccoli Bake with Toasted Almonds 42

cereal

Apple Strudel Breakfast Cereal 13

Blueberry Flax Hot Cereal 13

Hot Cranberry Date Cereal 14

Maple Walnut Cereal 14

Overnight Quinoa Cereal 17

Piña Colada Quinoa 17

Quick Peaches-and-Cream Breakfast Cereal 16

Raisin Pudding Breakfast Porridge 15

Raisin Spice Cereal 15

Super Fiber Cereal 16

Ultimate Granola, The 18

cheddar

Broccoli Cheese Soup 62

Black Bean Quinoa Quesadillas 41

Cheddar Cheese Bread (variation) 151

Cheese and Spinach Frittata 107

Cheese Ball 38

Chicken Broccoli Casserole 81

Easy Cheesy Sauce 39

Jalapeño Cheddar Pepper Scramble 26

Mexican Casserole 111

Quinoa Veggie Bake 109

Southwestern Quinoa 110

Vegetable Cheddar Quiche 106

cheese

Apple Cinnamon Cheesecake 155

Bocconcini and Oregano Salad 47

Broccoli Cheese Soup 62

Broccoli Goat Cheese Soufflé 103

Cheddar Cheese Bread (variation) 151

Cheese and Spinach Frittata 107

Cheese Ball 38

cheese sauce (Quinoa-Crusted Chicken with Sage) 86

Cheesy Spinach and Quinoa Stuffed Pasta 112

Chicken, Broccoli and Cheese Quinoa 191

Chicken Broccoli Casserole 81

Chocolate Cheesecake Brownies 146

Cucumber Gouda Sprout Sandwich 115

Easy Cheesy Sauce 39

Jalapeño Cheddar Pepper Scramble 26

Mexican Casserole 111

Quinoa Cheese Fruit Cup 188

Quinoa-Stuffed Chicken Breasts 87

Pomegranate, Almond and Feta Salad 50

Raspberry Cream Cheese Muffins 127

Rosemary Parmesan Bread (variation) 151

Soufflé Monterey 104

Southwestern Quinoa 110

Turkey-Stuffed Mozzarella Peppers 91

Vegetable Cheddar Quiche 106

Cheesecake, Apple Cinnamon 155

Cheesecake Brownies, Chocolate 146

chicken

Baked Chicken Nuggets 90

Chicken, Broccoli and Cheese Quinoa 191

Chicken, Quinoa and Apple Purée 187

Chicken Broccoli Casserole 81

Chicken Fried Quinoa 89

Chicken Sprout Salad Wrap 113

Chicken Vegetable Stew 75

Chicken Veggie Mélange 186

Ginger Edamame Quinoa (optional ingredient) 82

Hearty Beans and Greens Stew 75

Mango Chicken Quinoa 84

Moroccan Chicken on Quinoa 85

Quinoa-Crusted Chicken with Sage 86

Quinoa-Stuffed Chicken Breasts 87

Thai Cashew Chicken and Broccoli on Quinoa 88

chickpeas

Garden Burger, The 119

Quinoa Bean Salad 52

Quinoa Chickpea Salad 52

Quinoa Hummus 36

Pimento and Chickpea Quinoa 53

Chili 94

chocolate

Banana Chocolate Chip Babycakes 190

Chewy Chocolate Chip Cookies 138

Chocolate Almond Biscotti 139

Chocolate Cheesecake Brownies 146

Chocolate Fudge Cake 160

Chocolate Quinoa Crepes with Bananas 20

Chocolate Sugar Cookies 136

Chocolate Truffle Brownies 147

Decadent Chocolate Pudding 175

Double Chocolate Cookies 134

Moist Chocolate Cake 159

Pecan Chocolate Oatmeal Cookies 140

Quinoa Shortbread 132

chocolate (*continued*)

    Toffee Mocha Squares 145

    White Chocolate Macadamia Nut
        Cookies 135

Chowder, Quinoa, Leek and Corn 72

coconut, flaked

    Breakfast Fruit and Oatmeal Bars 32

    Healthy Cookies 131

    Raspberry Coconut Bars 149

    Ultimate Granola, The 18

coconut milk

    Curried Carrot Soup 64

    Piña Colada Quinoa 17

    Sweet Potato and Coconut Quinoa
        Soup 74

cookies. *See also* bars and squares

    Chewy Chocolate Chip Cookies 138

    Chocolate Almond Biscotti 139

    Chocolate Sugar Cookies 136

    Double Chocolate Cookies 134

    Ginger Molasses Cookies 143

    Healthy Cookies 131

    Oatmeal Raisin Cookies 141

    Peanut Butter Cookies 144

    Pecan Chocolate Oatmeal Cookies
        140

    Quinoa Shortbread 132

    White Chocolate Macadamia Nut
        Cookies 135

corn

    Quinoa, Leek and Corn Chowder 72

    Southwestern Quinoa 110

    Southwest Quinoa Salad 54

crabmeat (imitation)

    Easy Quinoa Temaki 100

    Sushi Salad 55

cranberries

    Cran-Apple Crisp 178

    Cranberry Orange Loaf 166

    Hot Cranberry Date Cereal 14

cream cheese

    Apple Cinnamon Cheesecake 155

    Carrot Cake 157

    Cheese Ball 38

    Chocolate Cheesecake Brownies 146

    Raspberry Cream Cheese Muffins 127

Crepes with Bananas, Chocolate Quinoa
    20

Crisp, Cran-Apple 178

Crumble, Strawberry Rhubarb 179

Crumble Crust, Very Berry Pie with 172

cucumber

    Cucumber Gouda Sprout Sandwich
        115

    Cucumber Mint Salad 45

    Fresh Cucumber and Toasted Almond
        Salad with Dill 48

Curried Carrot Soup 64

Dd

dates

    Caramel Date Cake 163

    Date Squares 148

    Hot Cranberry Date Cereal 14

dips

    Black Bean Nacho Dip 35

    Quinoa Bean Dip 35

    Quinoa Guacam-Óle! 36

    Quinoa Hummus 36

dried fruit

    Breakfast Fruit and Oatmeal Bars 32

Ee

Edamame Quinoa, Ginger 82

eggs

    Broccoli Goat Cheese Soufflé 103

    Cheese and Spinach Frittata 107

    Chicken Fried Quinoa 89

    Egg Salad Sandwich 116

    Jalapeño Cheddar Pepper Scramble
        26

    Light and Fluffy Eggs 26

    Quinoa Breakfast Burritos 27

    Ranch House Omelet 29

    Soufflé Monterey 104

    Spanikopita Frittata 108

    Tomato and Basil Crustless Quiche
        105

    Vegetable Cheddar Quiche 106

Ff

feta

    Greek Burgers 117

    Pomegranate, Almond and Feta Salad
        50

    Spanikopita Frittata 108

fish. *See also* crabmeat; shrimp

    Easy Quinoa Temaki 100

    Light Open-Faced Salmon Burgers
        118

    Roasted Vegetable Tilapia on Quinoa
        95

    Salmon and Red Quinoa on Asparagus
        with Lime Cilantro Sauce 97

    Sushi Salad 55

    Tasty Tuna Casserole 98

    Tuna Basil Sprout Sandwich 116

flax

    Berry Flax Bran Muffins 128

    Blueberry Flax Hot Cereal 13

    Blueberry Flax Pancakes (variation)
        24

Frittata, Cheese and Spinach 107

fruit

    Fine Fruit Smoothie 187

    Fresh Fruit Quinoa Parfaits 180

    Quinoa Cheese Fruit Cup 188

    Super Quinoa Fruit Purée 186

    Tropical Fruit Salad 31

Gg

Garlic Toasted Quinoa 56

Ginger Edamame Quinoa 82

Ginger Molasses Cookies 143

goat cheese

    Broccoli Goat Cheese Soufflé 103

    Quinoa-Stuffed Chicken Breasts 87

Gouda

    Cucumber Gouda Sprout Sandwich
        115

    Light Open-Faced Salmon Burgers
        118

    Quinoa-Crusted Chicken with Sage
        86

Granola, The Ultimate 18

Greek Burgers 117

Green Pea Soup, Mint and 69

Guacam-Óle!, Quinoa 36

Hh

Hash Browns, Golden 25

Healthy Cookies 131

Herb Biscuits 152

Hummus, Quinoa 36

Ii

Irish Soda Bread 151

Italian Wedding Soup 65

Jj

Jalapeño Cheddar Pepper Scramble 26

Ll

leek
    Leek and Potato Soup 66
    Quinoa, Leek and Corn Chowder 72
Lemon Blueberry Muffins 129
Lemon Poppy Seed Loaf 164
Lemon Quinoa Soup 66
lentils
    Garden Burger, The 119
    Mandarin Almond Salad 49
    Quinoa, Carrot and Lentil Stew 76
loaves
    Cranberry Orange Loaf 166
    Lemon Poppy Seed Loaf 164
    Pineapple Upside-Down Loaf 167
    Pumpkin Loaf 168

Mm

Macadamia Nut Cookies, White
    Chocolate 135
Mandarin Almond Salad 49
Mango Chicken Quinoa 84
Maple Bean Tarts 150
Maple Walnut Cereal 14
Meatballs, Santa Fe 40
Mexican Casserole 111
Minestrone Soup 68
mint
    Cucumber Mint Salad 45
    Mint and Green Pea Soup 69
Mocha Squares, Toffee 145
Molasses Cookies, Ginger 143
Moroccan Chicken on Quinoa 85
mozzarella
    Bocconcini and Oregano Salad 47
    Cheesy Spinach and Quinoa Stuffed
        Pasta 112
    Tomato and Basil Crustless Quiche
        105
    Turkey-Stuffed Mozzarella Peppers
        91
muffins
    Berry Flax Bran Muffins 128
    Carrot Spice Muffins 126
    Lemon Blueberry Muffins 129
    Raisin Bran Muffins 125
    Raspberry Cream Cheese Muffins 127
    Strawberry Banana Muffins 130
mushrooms
    Light and Creamy Mushroom Soup 67
    Mushroom and Herb Quinoa 43
    Mushroom Broccoli Quisotto 44
    Quinoa Veggie Bake 109
    Roasted Vegetable Tilapia on Quinoa
        95
    Stuffed Mushrooms 39

Nn

Nacho Dip, Black Bean 35

Oo

Oatmeal Bars, Breakfast Fruit and 32
Oatmeal Cookies, Pecan Chocolate 140
Oatmeal Raisin Cookies 141
Omelet, Ranch House 29

Pp

pancakes
    Banana Chocolate Chip Babycakes
        190
    Blueberry Flax Pancakes (variation)
        24
    Pumpkin Pancakes 23
    Quinoa Pancakes 24
Parfaits, Fresh Fruit Quinoa 180
pasta
    Cheesy Spinach and Quinoa Stuffed
        Pasta 112
peaches
    Quick Peaches-and-Cream Breakfast
        Cereal 16
peanut butter
    Peanut Butter and Banana Pudding
        176
    Peanut Butter Cookies 144
peas
    Mint and Green Pea Soup 69
Pecan Chocolate Oatmeal Cookies 140
Pecan Pumpkin Pie, Caramel 171
Pepper Shrimp Quinoa 99
Peruvian Peppered Steak on Quinoa 93
pie
    Basic Pie Crust 169
    Basic Tart Crust 169
    Caramel Pecan Pumpkin Pie 171
    Very Berry Pie with Crumble Crust
        172
Pimento and Chickpea Quinoa 53
pineapple
    Piña Colada Quinoa 17
    Pineapple Upside-Down Loaf 167
    Tropical Beach Smoothie 31
    Tropical Fruit Salad 31
Pizza Crust, Outrageously Quick and Easy
    120
Pomegranate, Almond and Feta Salad 50
Poppy Seed Loaf, Lemon 164
pork
    Chicken Fried Quinoa (optional
        ingredient) 89
    Ginger Edamame Quinoa (optional
        ingredient) 82
    Pork Chops on Quinoa, Apple-Glazed
        92
Porridge, Raisin Pudding Breakfast 15
Potage, Buffalo Quinoa 78
potatoes and sweet potatoes
    Beef and Sweet Potato Tagine on
        Quinoa 77
    Buffalo Quinoa Potage 78
    Dill Potato Salad 49
    Golden Hash Browns 25
    Leek and Potato Soup 66
    Perfect Baked Potato, The 122
    Sweet Potato and Coconut Quinoa
        Soup 74
pudding
    Caramelized Banana Pudding 173
    Creamy Quinoa Pudding 174
    Decadent Chocolate Pudding 175
    Peanut Butter and Banana Pudding
        176
    Raisin Pudding Breakfast Porridge 15
pumpkin
    Caramel Pecan Pumpkin Pie 171
    Pumpkin Loaf 168
    Pumpkin Pancakes 23

Qq

Quesadillas, Black Bean Quinoa 41
quiche
    Tomato and Basil Crustless Quiche
        105
    Vegetable Cheddar Quiche 106
quinoa, basic preparation of 4
    cooking ratios and yields 6, 183–4
    microwave oven 8
    rice steamer 6
    rinsing 4
    simmer and set 4

quinoa, basic preparation of (*continued*)
  slow cooker 8
  sprouts 6, 56
quinoa, health benefits of 2–3, 10
quinoa, nutritional content of 2–3, 10
quinoa, storage 4
quinoa flakes 4, 183–84
quinoa flour 3, 4, 184

Rr
raisins
  Oatmeal Raisin Cookies 141
  Raisin Bran Muffins 125
  Raisin Pudding Breakfast Porridge 15
  Raisin Spice Cereal 15
Ranch House Omelet 29
raspberries
  Berry Flax Bran Muffins 128
  Raspberry Cake 168
  Raspberry Coconut Bars 149
  Raspberry Cream Cheese Muffins 127
  Super Fiber Cereal 16
red peppers, roasted
  Roasted Red Pepper Tomato Soup 70
  Supreme Turkey Sprout Sandwich 113
  Tuna Basil Sprout Sandwich 116
Rhubarb Crumble, Strawberry 179
Roasted Red Pepper Tomato Soup 70
Roasted Vegetable Tilapia on Quinoa 95

Ss
salad
  Asian Sprout Salad 45
  Bocconcini and Oregano Salad 47
  Cucumber Mint Salad 45
  Dill Potato Salad 49
  Fresh Cucumber and Toasted Almond
    Salad with Dill 48
  Mandarin Almond Salad 49
  Pimento and Chickpea Quinoa 53
  Pomegranate, Almond and Feta Salad
    50
  Quinoa Bean Salad 52
  Quinoa Chickpea Salad 52
  Quinoa Tabbouleh 37
  Southwest Quinoa Salad 54
  Sunny Summer Salad 54
  Sushi Salad 55
  Tomato Quinoa Salad 55
  Tropical Fruit Salad 31

salmon
  Light Open-Faced Salmon Burgers
    118
  Salmon and Red Quinoa on Asparagus
    with Lime Cilantro Sauce 97
sandwiches
  Chicken Sprout Salad Wrap 113
  Cucumber Gouda Sprout Sandwich
    115
  Egg Salad Sandwich 116
  Supreme Turkey Sprout Sandwich 113
  Tuna Basil Sprout Sandwich 116
sauces
  cheese sauce 86
  Easy Cheesy Sauce 39
  lime cilantro sauce 97
Shortbread, Quinoa 132
shrimp
  Chicken Fried Quinoa (optional
    ingredient) 89
  Ginger Edamame Quinoa (optional
    ingredient) 82
  Pepper Shrimp Quinoa 99
smoothies
  Blueberry Vanilla Smoothie 30
  Fine Fruit Smoothie 187
  Strawberry Shake 30
  Tropical Beach Smoothie 31
soufflé
  Broccoli Goat Cheese Soufflé 103
  Soufflé Monterey 104
soup
  Beef Vegetable Quinoa Soup 61
  Black Bean Soup 59
  Broccoli Cheese Soup 62
  Chicken Vegetable Stew 75
  Chilled Avocado Soup 63
  Curried Carrot Soup 64
  Dill Beet Soup 65
  Hearty Beans and Greens Stew 75
  Italian Wedding Soup 65
  Leek and Potato Soup 66
  Lemon Quinoa Soup 66
  Light and Creamy Mushroom Soup 67
  Minestrone Soup 68
  Mint and Green Pea Soup 69
  Quinoa, Carrot and Lentil Stew 76
  Quinoa, Leek and Corn Chowder 72
  Roasted Red Pepper Tomato Soup 70
  Rustic Vegetable Soup 73

Sweet Potato and Coconut Quinoa
  Soup 74
Southwestern Quinoa 110
Southwest Quinoa Salad 54
Spanikopita Frittata 108
spinach
  Cheese and Spinach Frittata 107
  Cheesy Spinach and Quinoa Stuffed
    Pasta 112
  Pomegranate, Almond and Feta Salad
    50
  Spanikopita Frittata 108
sprouts (quinoa)
  Asian Sprout Salad 45
  Chicken Sprout Salad Wrap 113
  Cucumber Gouda Sprout Sandwich
    115
  Dill Potato Salad 49
  Egg Salad Sandwich 116
  nutritional value 6
  Quinoa Bean Salad (variation) 52
  Quinoa Sprouts 56
  Supreme Turkey Sprout Sandwich 113
  Tuna Basil Sprout Sandwich 116
squares. *See* bars and squares
Steak on Quinoa, Peruvian Peppered 93
stew. *See also* soup
  Beef and Sweet Potato Tagine on
    Quinoa 77
  Buffalo Quinoa Potage 78
  Chicken Vegetable Stew 75
  Hearty Beans and Greens Stew 75
  Quinoa, Carrot and Lentil Stew 76
strawberries
  Natural Strawberry Quinoa Yogurt 191
  Strawberry Banana Muffins 130
  Strawberry Rhubarb Crumble 179
  Strawberry Shake 30
Stuffed Mushrooms 39
Stuffing, Savory 44
sushi
  Easy Quinoa Temaki 100
  Sushi Salad 55
sweet potatoes. *See* potatoes and sweet
  potatoes

Tt
Tabbouleh, Quinoa 37
Tagine on Quinoa, Beef and Sweet Potato
  77

tarts. *See also* pie
    Basic Pie Crust 169
    Basic Tart Crust 169
    Maple Bean Tarts 150
Thai Cashew Chicken and Broccoli on
    Quinoa 88
Tilapia on Quinoa, Roasted Vegetable 95
Toasted Quinoa, Garlic 56
toffee
    Apple Toffee Cake 156
    Toffee Mocha Squares 145
tofu
    Chicken Fried Quinoa (optional
        ingredient) 89
    Easy Quinoa Temaki (optional
        ingredient) 100
    Ginger Edamame Quinoa (optional
        ingredient) 82
tomato
    Bocconcini and Oregano Salad 47
    Roasted Red Pepper Tomato Soup 70
    Tomato and Basil Crustless Quiche
        105
    Tomato Quinoa Salad 55
Truffle Brownies, Chocolate 147
tuna
    Tasty Tuna Casserole 98
    Tuna Basil Sprout Sandwich 116
turkey
    Baked Chicken Nuggets (optional
        ingredient) 90
    Chicken Sprout Salad Wrap (optional
        ingredient) 113
    Chili (optional ingredient) 94
    Italian Wedding Soup 65
    Santa Fe Meatballs 40
    Supreme Turkey Sprout Sandwich 113
    Turkey-Stuffed Mozzarella Peppers
        91

Vv
vegetables
    Beef Vegetable Quinoa Soup 61
    Cauliflower and Broccoli Bake with
        Toasted Almonds 42
    Chicken Vegetable Stew 75
    Chicken Veggie Mélange 186
    Healthy Quinoa Vegetable Purée 185
    Hearty Beans and Greens Stew 75
    Minestrone Soup 68

    Quinoa Veggie Bake 109
    Ranch House Omelet 29
    Roasted Vegetable Tilapia on Quinoa
        95
    Rustic Vegetable Soup 73
    Vegetable Cheddar Quiche 106

Ww
Waffles 19
Walnut Cereal, Maple 14
White Chocolate Macadamia Nut Cookies
    135
Wrap, Chicken Sprout Salad 113

Yy
Yogurt, Natural Strawberry Quinoa 191

ACKNOWLEDGMENTS

We thank our husbands, Ian Green and Paul Hemming, for their immense support and delightful, neverending humor, especially in regard to our cooking. Alyssa and Sydney are the most splendidly enthusiastic—and honest—food testers. We also dedicate this book to our grandparents, Esther Friesen and her late husband George and our late grandmother Florence Runkvist, for passing along their knowledge of nature and wholesome food and their love of the land.

Along the way we have received both tremendous guidance and encouragement for this project. Thank you to our father, Swen Runkvist, for his unconditional support. Also, our uncle, Robert Friesen, was an important catalyst for this book as he is the original reason Patricia first began to pursue gluten-free recipes, which led to her discovery of quinoa. We must acknowledge Jill Howell for introducing Patricia to quinoa. Thank you also to Caroline Connolly, Carolyn Botin, Claire Burnett, Fay Lewis, Joan Streadwick, Jocelyn Campanaro, Jodi Bates, Joe Dutcheshen, Joy Hemming, Dr. Laurie Scanlin, the Lewis family, Mary Decelles, Dr. Michael Eskin, Michael Dutcheshen, Onalee Orchard, Paul Challen, Richard Meunier, Robert McCullough, Sara Busby and all of our friends and family. Thank you to all the fantastic people we have met on this adventure. —PG and CH

Importantly, for her vision for this book, all of her brilliant ideas and her everyday courage, this book must contain a special appreciation for my sister and coauthor, Patricia, always affectionately referred to as "Sista." —CH